101
OFFENSIVE
SOFTBALL DRILLS

Sue Enquist
James A. Peterson

ISBN: 158518-347-4
Library of Congress Number: 00-108324

Book layout and cover design: Paul W. Lewis
Front cover photo: courtesy UCLA Sports Information Department

Coaches Choice
P.O. Box 1828
Monterey, CA 93942
www.coacheschoice.com

DEDICATION

I would like to dedicate this book to my dad and mom, Bill and Jane Enquist for teaching me that hard work and a positive attitude are the keys to success. To my sister, Becky Morey, for her eternal support and spiritual inspiration. To my best friend growing up and my role model, my brother, Bill Enquist, Jr. for always picking me first in street ball. You built my confidence and taught me how to be a winner. I love you all.

ACKNOWLEDGMENTS

I would like to express my appreciation and deep gratitude to Sharron Backus (UCLA head coach 1976-1996) who was my coach at UCLA and who provided me with this wonderful career of coaching at UCLA. It was so enjoyable playing for you, and it was an honor coaching with you. You have taught me so much for which I will always be indebted to you.

I would also like to thank all the Bruins throughout UCLA Softball history for building and sustaining the rich tradition of success in the classroom and on the ball field. Special thanks to Dot Richardson, for her unwavering support and loyalty to me and the Bruin softball program.

Thank you to all the Bruins below for the use of their action shots in this book: Dot Richardson, Yvonne Guiterrez, Lyndsey Klein, Julie Adams and especially Jen Brundage, who performed most of these drills and provided photographic diagrams.

Lastly, Dr. Jim Peterson, publisher of Coaches Choice, for your friend-ship throughout the years and support throughout this project.

CONTENTS

Instructional drills are like medicine. The proper prescription can help a player in innumerable ways. The coach, however, had the ultimate responsibility to administer the "medicine" at the right time, in the right amount, and in the right way.

In that regard, all drills should be conducted in a learning atmosphere where every player is given every opportunity to be successful. When an athlete does well, she should be praised. When and athlete's performance does not measure up to expectations, she should be given constructive feedback that enables her to redirect her efforts in such a manner to achieve the desired change.

The technique of skill being stressed in a particular drill should be *over emphasized.* Coaches should insist and strive for perfection in every drill, by every player, on every repetition. Players and coaches should be patient for success to arrive. Changing muscle memory takes a high volume of drill repetition.

The 101 drills included in this book are designed to improve the primary skills involved in offensive softball—hitting, bunting, baserunning, and sliding. I have field-tested and applied each of these drills over the course of my career. If in the process of using the drills presented in this book, coaches are better able to develop the abilities of their players, then the effort to write *101 Offensive Softball Drills* will have been well worthwhile.

___Sue Enquist

- *Stride phase:* Emphasize to the hitter that she land on the big toe of her stride foot. This will enable her to keep her weight balanced, towards the plate and not "falling away" from the plate.

- *Two-strike stance:* During drill sessions and practice, rehearse "two-strike" stance. The hitter chokes up slightly, opens her hips to the pitcher slightly, and widens her stance slightly. At the same time, she changes her mindset to making contact with a short, compact swing, with a bigger strike zone. This strategy helps build their confidence when they arrive in a two-strike count. Instead of panicking, they realize they have practiced this during the week prior to the game.

- *Look for a pitch below the hands:* This helps the hitters lay off a rise ball thrower who brings the ball into the zone, but by the time it reaches the plate it is a "ball."

- *Bunt the outside pitch fair:* The most common problem with hitters bunting the outside pitch is they make successful contact, but the ball goes foul. During practice, set the pitching machine on the outside part of the plate. Emphasize to the hitters to "catch" the "outside" part of the ball (which is the right side of the ball, for a right handed batter, as it arrives in the contact zone) with the barrel of the bat and bring the knob in towards the belly button.

- *Increase focus on batting-T hitting:* Require the hitters to keep their eyes/head on the tee *after* they hit the ball.

- *Establish "game-like" batting-T hitting:* Each hitter has a partner who stands on the other side of the sock net and pitches the imaginary ball to the hitter who focuses on the pitcher's release point and then the hitter switches her focus to the batting T and hits the ball.

- *Fine focus on batting-T hitting:* Encourage hitter to fine focus on three or four seams on the ball, which is sitting on the batting T and *not* just the "whole ball."

- *Hitters "stand in" in the bullpen:* Whenever the pitchers are carrying out their pitching workout. Have the hitters "stand in" without swinging and work on picking up the spin and rotation of the different pitches.

- *Hitters "stand in" and call out "yes" for a strike and "no" for a ball:* The hitters are required to call out "yes" on a strike and "no" on a ball. This can be done in the bullpen or as the on-deck batter who is placed behind the catcher in live batting practice and she is protected by a safety net but can see the pitcher's release point and whether the pitch is a strike or a ball.

- *Establish "timing of your stride":* When on deck, the hitter should base her stride timing off of the pitcher's quickest pitch. Therefore, she will always be prepared for the quickest pitch. As the off speed pitch arrives, the stride timing is still the same, but, the hands must "stay back" slightly longer until the ball reaches the "contact zone."

- *Understand the volume of swings necessary to change muscle memory:* Remember that most hitters have established muscle memory with thousands of swings. Be patient and understand that it takes thousands of swings to "change" muscle memory and form "good" hitting mechanics.

- *Emphasize the proper sequence in which the front arm (which many times causes the casting or looping swing) unlocks/extends in the swing phase:* Shoulder first, then the elbow unlock and then the wrist.

- *To improve the hitters "compact swing":* Instruct the hitters to "throw" their hands *inside* the path of the ball. By doing so, the hitter won't cast her hands outward and create a looping swing.

- *Increase forearm and wrist strength:* The lower extremities of the arm are very important in hitting. Utilize a ball bucket *full* of *rice* and instruct the hitter to try and reach the bottom of the bucket (this is very challenging and fun). Build up their repetitions. Start with three sets of three repetitions (one repetition=digging to the bottom to fatigue).

- *Analyzing the hitter's swing:* As a coach, don't start analyzing the hitter's swing until she is warmed up and has established her normal swing and rhythm.

PHOTOGRAPHIC BREAKDOWN OF HITTING

STRIDE/LOAD PHASE

There is a slight cocking of the knee inward and there is some slight movement of the elbows and wrists backwards (loading). Emphasis that the front elbow should cock back to approximately the midline of the body. Wrists remain flexed and barrel remains in a good launching position: no casting or dipping of the barrel.

STANCE PHASE

Both eyes level and focused on pitcher's release point.

Chin over front shoulder.

Front shoulder closed to pitcher.

Flex in shoulder, elbow and wrist.

Bat positions vary, yet all are in an excellent launching position.

Slight bend in hips and knees.

Good athletic position—weight is balanced.

SWING PHASE

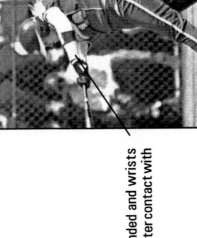

Head down on the ball.

Chin finishing over back shoulder.

Front shoulder remains "in" prior to contact.

Elbows are extending, flexed wrists in palm-up/palm-down position just prior to contact.

Arms extended and wrists extended after contact with the ball.

Upon contact the foot and leg remain firm (this keeps the hitter balanced throughout the swing). This allows the hitter to "remain back and behind the ball on contact."

SWING PHASE/FOLLOW THROUGH

Hips have snapped open from the back foot pivot. Back foot has pivoted. Back foot rotates and heel lifts off the ground.

Notice the excellent vertical "stacking" of right shoulder, right hip and right knee. this hitter is in good balance throughout the swing.

Lead front foot strides at a 90 degree angle to the pitchers. By doing so, the hitters weight doesn't "spin" away from the contact area.

Weight Distribution During the Swing

During the swing the hitter should keep the weight of her body on the balls of her feet. Just over half of the body weight should be over the back foot.

Upon the stride phase, approximately 70% of the body weight is over the inside of the back foot. This weight will transfer forward as the bat travels forward through the ball. At this time, it is important the hitter has a "firm front leg" upon contact. This will keep her weight balanced throughout the swing and not forward.

After contact, the front leg "releases" and there is a slight bend in the front leg again during follow through.

Depending on the hitter's swing arc, some hitters will finish their swings high at the base of the neck, while others will finish across the top of the shoulders and shoulder blades.

Emphasize that the barrel should take a *direct* path to the ball. During a *level* swing, the hands remain higher than the pitch and the barrel remains higher than the hands. On the low pitch, the barrel will be below the hands.

NOTE: I have addressed the core areas of the swing and the important phases that occur. There are variations in each person's swing. No two hitters look the same. For example, stride distance, bat angles, and hand position can vary from player to player.

CHAPTER 1

LOWER BODY HITTING DRILLS

Drill #1: Stride Drill

Objective: To practice striding properly while hitting.

Equipment Needed: One bat per player.

Description: The players should spread out along one foul line and assume their regular stance with the bat. Each player practices striding into an imaginary pitch at her own pace, taking a low, quick step forward. The coach should move from player to player and make individual corrections as needed.

Coaching Points:

➡ The coach should make sure the hitter does not move her weight too far forward, which causes her to throw her hips forward.

➡ The coach should emphasize keeping the lead foot closed while striding so the hitter does not open up too soon.

Photo 1.1 "Stance" position.

Photo 1.2 "Stride" position—notice her body remains centered (not leaning back or forward) and her stride foot remains closed.

Drill #2: Thera-band® Strides

Objective: To practice striding properly while hitting.

Equipment Needed: A bat, glove, and Thera-band® (or a large rubberband) per player.

Description: The Thera-band® is tied around the front toes of each player to provide resistance and prevent overstriding. Each hitter places her glove on the ground to simulate home plate, and assumes her regular stance with the bat. At her own pace, she practices striding into an imaginary pitch. The coach should circulate among the players, making corrections where necessary.

Coaching Points:

➡ The coach should emphasize keeping the lead foot closed while striding so the hitter does not open up too soon.

➡ The coach should emphasize a short, quick stride and make sure the player does not move her weight too far forward.

Photo 2.1 Stride phase.

Photo 2.2 Notice that her lead foot is closed.

Drill #3: Shackles

Objective: To practice striding properly while hitting.

Equipment Needed: A bat, glove, and set of hitting shackles per player.

Description: The hitting shackles are placed on each hitter's ankles and adjusted to fit her ideal stride. The hitter places her glove on the ground to simulate home plate and assumes her regular stance with the ball. At her own pace, she practices striding into an imaginary pitch. The shackles will keep her from overstriding. The coach should circulate among the players and make corrections where necessary.

Coaching Points:

➡ The coach should emphasize keeping the lead foot closed while striding so the player does not open up too soon.

➡ The coach should also make sure the hitter does not shorten her stride too much trying to ovoid overstriding.

Drill #4: Stride Box

Objective: To practice striding properly while hitting.

Equipment Needed: A bat and a four-inch-deep wooden box.

Description: This drill begins with a player taking a position in the box. She should place her back foot in a position that barely allows her to take her normal short, quick stride without hitting the front of the box. At her own pace, she practices striding into an imaginary pitch, concentrating on sound fundamental techniques. The coach should observe the hitter and make corrections when necessary.

Coaching Points:

➡ The coach should make sure the players keep their weight back and their lead foot closed while striding.

➡ Since the hitter can't begin pivot phase until her stride foot lands, it is important the hitter has a short stride.

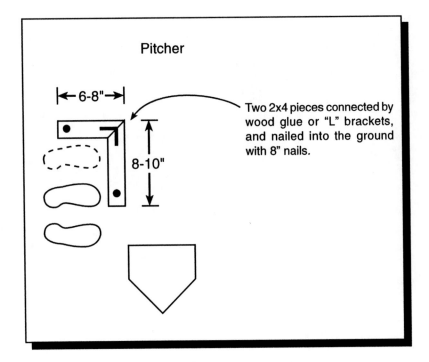

Drill #5: Balloon/Ball Drill

Objective: To emphasize the importance of taking a short stride.

Equipment Needed: A bat, glove, and deflated volleyball or soccer ball (inflated balloons can be used indoors) for every player participating.

Description: This drill begins with the player placing her glove on the ground to simulate home plate and assuming her normal stance with the bat. The deflated ball is placed between the player's upper thighs and she practices taking short, quick strides. If her stride is too wide, the ball will drop to the ground. The coach should observe the players and make adjustments in technique where necessary.

Coaching Point: The coach should emphasize keeping the weight centered and the lead foot closed while striding.

Photo 5.1 The stance.

Photo 5.2 The stride—note her balance; her weight is centered.

Drill #6: Hip Pivot Drill

Objective: To improve the hitter's ability to properly use her hips while hitting.

Equipment Needed: A bat and glove for every player participating.

Description: Each player places her glove on the ground to simulate home plate and assumes her regular stance, placing the bat on or slightly off her shoulder. The player concentrates on an imaginary pitch, and as the ball "arrives," she rotates her hips <u>instead of swinging</u>. She then rolls up on her back foot and drives her hips through the ball. This places her body in position to help her hands drive through the hitting zone. The coach may also wish to have the hitter rotate her hips as if hitting to the opposite field a designated number of times, and then practice to the power field.

Coaching Point: The coach should make sure the hitter pivots on the ball of her rear foot and thrusts her hips through the imaginary ball. During the entire drill the batter is keeping her hands back. The upper body is not involved in the drill.

Drill #7: Hip Rotation Drill

Objective: To improve the hitter's ability to open the hips quickly; to improve the player's understanding of the importance of hip rotation to the swing.

Equipment Needed: A bat and glove for every player participating.

Description: Each player places her glove on the ground to simulate home plate and then places a bat behind her back at waist level with the head of the bat pointed away from the imaginary pitcher's mound. Holding the bat in a horizontal position, the hitter assumes her regular stance. She concentrates on an imaginary pitch and assumes a position as if she has already completed her stride. As the imaginary pitch arrives, she pulls the bat with her dominant hand so the head of the bat is pointed toward the imaginary pitcher. While she is opening her hips, she rolls up on her back foot. Once the basic techniques have been mastered, the hitter should practice striding into the imaginary pitch while opening her hips and pulling on the bat. She uses the bat to help her hips drive through the pitch.

Coaching Point: The coach should emphasize pivoting on the ball of the rear foot.

Photo 7.1 Stance.

Photo 7.2 Stride.

Photo 7.3 Pivot. Notice the back foot turns and the heel raises of the ground.

Photo 7.4 Pivot with the ball. Note that hitting the ball is normally not that deep in the zone.

CHAPTER 2

UPPER BODY
HITTING DRILLS

Drill #8: Wrist-Roll Drill

Objective: To strengthen the player's hands, wrists, and forearms.

Equipment Needed: A horizontal bar with a weight suspended from a rope attached to the middle (a wooden dowel, rope and weighted which vary in lbs. 5, 10, 15, etc.).

Description: The player grasps the bar with both hands, holding it at waist level (be sure to keep your elbows next to your body). The suspended weight should not touch the ground. The player curls her wrists up and down to raise and lower the weight. The drill continues for a prescribed period of time or until a designated number of repetitions has been completed.

Coaching Point: The coach should vary the amount of weight and/or number of repetitions according to the strength of each player. Be sure the player keeps the arm position at a 90° angle and emphasize just wrist action and not forearm movement up and down.

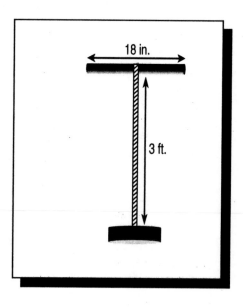

Drill #9: Bat-Twirl Drill

Objective: To increase bat control and develop hand, wrist, and forearm strength.

Equipment Needed: A bat for every player participating.

Description: The player extends her arms in front of her body with a slight bend in the arms. She holds the bat in a vertical position and begins to rotate clockwise in a tight circle, gradually increasing the speed of the bat head. After a designated period of time, the player twirls the bat in a counterclockwise direction until the drill ends.

Coaching Points:

➡ The coach should emphasize bat speed and keeping the twirls in a tight circle.

➡ Increase players' repetition gradually. By doing so, you will eliminate joint injury.

Drill #10: Bat and Forth Drill

Objective: To increase bat control and develop hand, wrist, and forearm strength.

Equipment Needed: A bat for every player participating.

Description: The player extends her arms in front of her body with a slight bend in the arms and holds the bat in a vertical position. She then begins to rock the bat from left to right, stopping the bat's downward arc at waist level, and gradually increases the bat speed. The drill continues for a designated period of time or until a prescribed number of repetitions is completed.

Coaching Points:

➡ The coach should emphasize bat speed and control, paying careful attention to where the player stops the bat on the downward arc.

➡ Increase players' repetition gradually. By doing so, you will eliminate joint injury.

Drill #11: Wrist Figure-Eights

Objective: To increase bat control and develop hand, wrist, and forearm strength.

Equipment Needed: A bat for every player participating.

Description: The player holds the bat in a vertical position out in front of her body with her arms slightly bent. She begins to rotate the bat to create an imaginary figure eight in the air, gradually increasing the bat speed. After a designated period of time or number of repetitions, the player reverses the direction of the bat and creates the figure eight in the other direction until the drill is complete.

Coaching Points:

➡ The coach should emphasize bat speed and control, making certain the figure-eighties are executed properly.

➡ The players' repetitions should be increased gradually, in order to prevent a joint injury from occuring.

Drill #12: Both Hand Wrist Snaps

Objective: To increase hand, wrist, and forearm strength.

Equipment Needed: A bat for every player participating.

Description: The drill begins with the player holding the bat in her back hand. She then swings the bat, starting the swing just prior to the wrist roll. She snaps the wrist through and quickly returns the bat to the starting position. She repeats the process as quickly as possible until time has expired or a designated number of repetitions have been completed, then moves the bat to her lead hand and repeats the drill.

Coaching Points:

➡ The coach should emphasize gripping the bat properly and snapping the wrist quickly.

➡ The coach should stress performing the drill quickly without sacrificing proper technique.

➡ The players' repetitions should be increased gradually, in order to prevent a joint injury.

Drill #13: Two-Hand Wrist Snaps

Objective: To increase hand, wrist, and forearm strength.

Equipment Needed: A bat for every player participating.

Description: The drill begins with the player holding the bat with both hands using her normal batting grip. She then takes a swing, starting the swing just prior to the wrist roll. She snaps her wrists through and quickly returns the bat to the starting position. She repeats the process as quickly as possible until time has expired or a designated number of repetitions have been completed.

Coaching Points:

➡ The coach should emphasize gripping the bat properly and snapping the wrist through quickly.

➡ The coach should stress performing the drill quickly without sacrificing proper technique.

Drill #14: Bat Throws

Objective: To improve the mechanics of the slow barrel hitter; to emphasize the importance of the wrist snap in the swing.

Equipment Needed: A bat and net for every player participating. This drill may be done at an open field where there aren't other players in the area.

Description: Each player assumes her normal batting stance approximately 10 feet from the net, with the net in line with an imaginary pitcher's mound. The hitter swings at an imaginary pitch, concentrating on throwing the barrel of the bat into the net. She releases her grip and allows the bat to fly into the net, barrel first. The drill is repeated for a predetermined number of repetitions.

Coaching Points:

➡ The coach should emphasize snapping the wrists quickly and getting the barrel of the bat out in front.

➡ The coach should be sure that no other players are in the vicinity whle bats are being thrown.

Drill #15: Bat Rolls

Objective: To increase hand, wrist, and forearm strength; to improve bat speed and control.

Equipment Needed: A bat for every player participating.

Description: The player assumes a stance with her hips facing an imaginary pitcher, then swings the bat, starting the swing just prior to the wrist roll. She rolls the bat forward and backward, completing a full swing by touching both shoulders with the bat. She should execute the swing using only her wrists and forearms. The drill is performed for a designated period of time or until a predetermined number of repetitions has been completed. The drill can also be performed with the hitter beginning in her normal batting stance.

Coaching Points:

➡ The coach should remind the hitter to keep her hands and wrists relaxed during the drill.

➡ The coach should emphasize performing the drill quickly without sacrificing proper technique. The player should feel a torso

➡ The player should feel a torso stretch (hips are open to pitcher, but arms are still back) prior to swing. This will enable them to "feel" keeping the front side closed to the pitcher as long as possible.

CHAPTER 3

COMBINATION HITTING DRILLS

Drill #16: Fence Behind the Hitter

Objective: To eliminate a hitter's tendency to shift her weight backward before moving forward.

Equipment Needed: A bat and a fence (or wall).

Description: The coach should position the player in her normal stance just in front of a fence or wall. The hitter concentrates on an imaginary pitch and swings through the ball. If she shifts her weight backward before attacking the ball, she will hit the wall with the bat, providing her with instant negative feedback. The drill is performed for a specific period of time or until a designated number of repetitions is completed. The repetitive nature of this drill will help eliminate the improper weight shift.

Coaching Points:

➡ The coach should position the hitter in such a way that only a proper swing can be performed without striking the fence.

➡ The coach should emphasize performing the drill quickly without sacrificing proper technique.

➡ The coach should emphasize that the hands don't extend backwards in the stride pase. The wrist and arms remain cocked in the stride phase.

Photo 16.1 "Right" way.

Photo 16.2 "Wrong" way—she shifted her weight before attacking the ball.

Drill #17: One Eye Blind

Objective: To improve the hitter's ability to utilize both eyes during the swing.

Equipment Needed: A bat and an eye patch for each player participating.

Description: Each player assumes her normal batting stance with her front eye covered by the patch. She then swings at imaginary pitches, concentrating on visualizing the release point as the imaginary ball leaves the imaginary pitcher's hand. This forces the batter to turn her head so her back eye can see the release point, which will make her utilize both eyes when hitting. The drill should be done for a specified period of time or until a designated number of repetitions is completed.

Coaching Point: The coach should emphasize the importance of maintaining a fundamentally sound swing and keeping the head in a position where both eyes can see the ball.

Drill #18: Resistance Drill

Objective: To increase the power of the swing.

Equipment Needed: A bat for every pair of players participating.

Description: The players should be separated into pairs. One player assumes her normal batting stance and swings at imaginary pitches. Her partner places both hands firmly on the barrel of the bat and provides resistance as the hitter swings through the strike zone. The partner should walk around the hitter to allow her to complete her swing. This forces the hitter to use more force when executing her practice swings and will increase her bat speed and power through the hitting zone when the resistance is removed. After a specified period of time or number of repetitions, the players switch roles and repeat the drill.

Coaching Points:

➡ The coach should observe the players and make corrections in hitting mechanics where necessary.

➡ The coach may choose to have the partner apply less force early in the drill and increase the resistance as the drill continues.

Photo 18.1

Photo 18.2

Photo 18.3

Photo 18.4

Drill #19: Self-Visualization Drill

Objective: To teach the player to improve and critique her own swing.

Equipment Needed: A bat for each player participating and as many full-length mirrors as possible.

Description: Each player should assume her normal batting stance facing the mirror and evaluate her stance, paying special attention to the position of her legs, hands, and bat. She should then turn sideways and repeat the process. Finally, she executes a series of practice swings, both sideways and facing the mirror, at imaginary pitches in all areas of the strike zone. The process of self-evaluation continues as she analyzes all phases of her swing. If the equipment is available, the coach may choose to record the players' swings with a video camera and have the players review their efforts on film.

Coaching Points:

➡ The coach should emphasize practicing proper techniques.

➡ The coach may have the hitter concentrate on a specific pitch location that has been giving her trouble.

➡ The team may be split into small groups based on the number of mirrors available, with one group performing the drill at a time.

Drill #20: Weighted-Bat Swings

Objective: To increase bat speed; to strengthen the hands, wrists, and forearms.

Equipment Needed: A weighted bat or doughnut for each player participating.

Description: The hitter assumes her normal stance using a weighted bat. The bat should be substantially heavier than the one she normally uses. She then concentrates on an imaginary pitch and swings through the ball. Despite the additional weight, she should concentrate on using proper hitting technique. This will increase bat speed when she returns to a normal bat. The drill should be performed for a set period of time or number of repetitions.

Coaching Point: The coach should observe all elements of the swing and stress performing the drill quickly.

Drill #21: Underloaded-Bat Swings

Objective: To improve bat control, to increase bat speed.

Equipment Needed: An underloaded bat for each player participating.

Description: The hitter assumes her normal stance with an underloaded bat. The bat should be substantially lighter than the one she normally uses. She then concentrates on an imaginary pitch and swings through the ball. She should focus on bat control, since the lighter bat will be more difficult to control while swinging. This will improve her bat control when she returns to her normal bat. This drill should be performed for a prescribed period of time or number of repetitions.

Coaching Point: The coach should emphasize proper mechanics and quick performance of the drill.

Photo 21.1 Swinging at a ball on a tee if the player is not sufficiently skilled for a tossed ball.

Photo 21.2 Swinging at a softball-sized wiffle ball.

Photo 21.3 Swinging at a baseball-sized wiffle ball.

Photo 21.4 Swinging at a golf ball-sized wiffle ball.

Drill #22: Tire Drill

Objective: To improve hitting mechanics; to condition all of the muscle groups used in hitting; to strengthen forearm and wrist strength.

Equipment Needed: A bat and a tire suspended on a rope.

Description: The tire should be suspended from a post or tree. The hitter assumes her normal batting stance at a distance from the tire that will allow her to complete a fully extended swing. She swings the bat at full speed, hitting the tire. It is critical that she drive through the tire with full force and complete her follow-through. The drill is performed for a pre-scribed period of time or number of repetitions. The resistance provided by the tire will help to strengthen the muscles used in hitting.

Coaching Points:

➡ The coach should emphasize proper hitting fundamentals, especially the follow-through.

➡ The coach should emphasize the wrist snap occurs after the barrel makes contact with the tire.

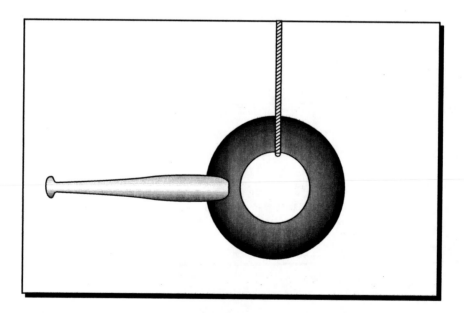

Diagram 22.1 The sweet part of the barrel should contact the outer edge of the tire. This contact area is on the side of the tire, NOT *on* the tire tread.

Drill #23: Fence in Front of the Hitter

Objective: To increase bat speed; to eliminate a sweeping swing.

Equipment Needed: A bat and a fence (or wall).

Description: The hitter assumes her normal batting stance facing a fence or wall approximately three feet in front of her. She should concentrate on an imaginary pitch and practice her normal swing. If she uses a sweeping swing, she will be provided with instant negative feedback when she hits the fence. This will help her hit inside pitches with the barrel of the bat instead of the handle. It will also teach her to keep her hands close to her body, which will increase her bat speed. The drill should be performed for a specified period of time or until a designated number of repetitions have been completed.

Coaching Points:

➡ It is important that the coach position the hitter at such a distance from the fence that only a proper swing can be performed without striking the fence.

➡ The coach should emphasize performing the drill quickly without sacrificing proper technique. Repetition is the key to success.

Photo 23.1 The knot of the bat on the belly button.

Photo 23.2 "Poor" swing— her hands are too far away from her body.

Photo 23.3 "Good" swing— she stayed compact and kept her hands inside the pitch.

Drill #24: Side-Corner Drill

Objective: To eliminate casting away from the body during the swing.

Equipment Needed: A bat, two walls (or fences) that form a corner.

Description: The hitter assumes her normal batting stance positioned in a corner of a room or fence at such a distance that there is just enough room to execute a proper swing. She then focuses on swinging at imaginary pitches. If she shifts her weight backward or lunges outward during the swing, she will hit one of the walls. The drill is performed for a specified period of time or until a designated number of swings is performed. The repetitive nature of this drill will help perfect the swing.

Coaching Points:

➡ The coach should position the hitter in such a way that only a proper swing can be executed without casting the hands outwards and striking one of the walls.

➡ The coach should emphasize performing the drill quickly without sacrificing proper technique.

Photo 24.1

Drill #25: Scarf Drill

Objective: To teach the batter to keep the front side of her body closed and down.

Equipment Needed: A bat and a scarf for each player participating (Note: in the photo below, a tennis ball was used).

Description: The hitter assumes her normal stance and a scarf is inserted under her front arm. The scarf is held in place as long as the hitter keeps her front side closed (down) while she swings. If she allows her front side to fly open, the scarf will drop to the ground. The drill is performed for a specified period of time or until a designated number of repetitions is completed.

Coaching Point: The coach should emphasize all elements of proper hitting technique, especially keeping the front arm closed (down) during the swing phase.

Photo 25.1

Drill #26: Blind Drill

Objective: To improve the hitter's balance throughout the swing.

Equipment Needed: A bat and blindfold for each player participating.

Description: The hitter assumes her normal batting stance with a blindfold covering both eyes. She concentrates on swinging at an imaginary pitch at normal speed. The blindfold makes it very easy for the hitter to lose her sense of balance. As she concentrates on maintaining her balance throughout her swing, the batting stroke will become more automatic. The drill is performed for a set period of time or number of repetitions.

Coaching Point: The coach should emphasize proper hitting fundamentals, especially balance and the proper shifting of weight.

Drill #27: Bat Stops

Objective: To enhance the batter's ability to make quick decisions and adjust on bad pitches.

Equipment Needed: A bat for each player participating.

Description: Each player takes full swings at imaginary pitches. As the drill progresses, the coach will command the hitter to stop her swing as if she had started to go after a bad pitch. The hitter must react quickly to stop the swing, increasing both bat control and the ability to make quick decisions. The drill is run for a specified period of time or a number of repetitions. Players can also be divided into pairs, with the hitter's partner giving the command to stop.

Coaching Point: The coach should emphasize the importance of full-speed practice swings to the learning process of the drill.

Drill #28: Quick-Swings Drill

Objective: To improve hitting mechanics; to strengthen and increase the quickness of the hands.

Equipment Needed: A bat for each player participating.

Description: Each player assumes her normal stance and takes full swings at imaginary pitches. The drill is run for a time period designated by the coach. The object is to take as many fundamentally correct swings as possible during the allotted time. The rapidity of the drill will help increase the player's hand strength and quickness.

Coaching Points:

➡ The coach should make sure proper techniques are not sacrificed for quickness during this drill.

➡ The coach should emphasize returning the bat quickly to the ready position after each swing.

Drill #29: No Stride Drill

Objective: To teach hitters to keep their hands back during their swing.

Equipment Needed: A bat for each player participating.

Description: The hitter assumes a position as if her stride has already occurred. She then visualizes an imaginary pitch and executes a series of practice swings. Starting the swing with the hips already open forces the hitter to keep her hands back. The drill is performed for a set period of time or until a designated number of repetitions has been completed.

Coaching Point: The coach should emphasize proper positioning of the hands and bat during the swing.

Drill #30: Rear Leg Drill

Objective: To teach players to keep their rear leg back when hitting.

Equipment Needed: A bat and a folding chair for each player participating.

Description: The player assumes her normal batting stance with her back leg pressed against a folding chair. She concentrates on an imaginary pitch and takes a series of practice swings. If her back leg has moved too far during the swing, there will be a large space between her leg and the chair. If her leg remains close to the chair, she has kept her leg back. This drill is performed for a set period of time or number of repetitions.

Coaching Points:

➡ The coach should observe the players and make corrections of hitting mechanics where necessary.

➡ This is a good drill to use with specific players who have trouble staying back when swinging.

CHAPTER 4

BATTING TEE DRILLS

Drill #31: One Knee—One Arm

Objective: To improve proper hitting mechanics; to increase hand, wrist, and forearm strength.

Equipment Needed: A bat, softballs, a batting tee, and a net.

Description: The batting tee is placed approximately 10 feet from the net. The player assumes a stance with her back knee on the ground and her front foot flat on the ground, creating approximately a 90-degree angle with her front leg. A softball is placed on the tee and the hitter grips the bat in her back hand and swings through the ball. The drill is repeated for a designated period of time, and then the hitter switches the bat to her front arm and performs the drill again.

Coaching Points:

➡ The coach should emphasize performing the drill quickly without sacrificing proper technique.

➡ The coach may increase the speed of the drill by using a partner to place balls on the tee.

➡ The coach should emphasize that the body remain "tall," unlocking the shoulder, elbow and wrist in that order upon hitting the ball.

Photo 31.1 Using a youth (18 oz.) bat.

Photo 31.2 Choking up on a regular bat.

Drill #32: One Knee—Both Arms

Objective: To improve hitting mechanics; to increase hand, wrist, and fore-arm strength.

Equipment Needed: A bat, softballs, a batting tee, and a net.

Description: The batting tee is placed approximately 10 feet from the net. The player assumes a stance with her back knee on the ground and her front foot flat on the ground, creating approximately a 90-degree angle with her front leg. A softball is placed on the tee and the hitter grips the bat with both hands in her normal batting position. She then takes a full swing through the ball, concentrating on proper technique. The drill is repeated for a designated time period or until a certain number of repetitions is completed.

Coaching Points:

➡ The coach should emphasize performing the drill quickly without sacrificing proper technique.

➡ The coach may increase the speed of the drill by using a partner to place balls on the tee.

➡ The coach should emphasize that the body remain "tall," unlocking the shoulder, elbow and wrist in that order upon hitting the ball.

Photo 32.1 Using a regular bat with both arms.

Drill #33: Pitch Location Drill

Objective: To develop the proper mechanics necessary to hit a pitch in any location and to all fields.

Equipment Needed: A bat, softballs, two batting tees, and a net.

Description: The batting tees are positioned with one high and inside, and the other low and outside. The hitter assumes her normal batting stance at an appropriate distance from the first tee. On command, she executes the proper swing necessary to pull the high-inside pitch and quickly returns to the ready position. As soon as she is ready, she hits the low-outside ball to the opposite field, adjusting her swing accordingly. The tee positions can be altered at the coach's discretion (high outside, low inside, inside-belt high, outside-belt high, etc.).

Coaching Points:

➡ The coach should emphasize concentrating on pitch location and using the proper mechanics necessary to hit the ball where it is pitched.

➡ The drill should be performed daily in the early part of the season and all elements of the swing should be critiqued. It is easier to spot flaws during tee work than live pitching.

Photo 33.1 Swinging at an inside pitch—just prior to hitting the ball.

Photo 33.2 Follow through—not hitting the outside pitch.

Photo 33.3 Swinging at an outside pitch—just prior to hitting the ball.

Photo 33.4 Follow through—not hitting the inside pitch.

Drill #34: Lead-Arm Swings

Objective: To teach hitters to properly extend the lead arm.

Equipment Needed: A bat, softballs, a batting tee, and a net.

Description: The player places a softball on the tee and assumes her normal stance, then removes her top hand from the bat and places it behind her back. She then swings through the ball, driving it into the net approximately 10 feet in front of her. She should concentrate on fully extending her lead arm and following all the way through. She performs the drill for a specified number of repetitions. The drill can be run without the tee by having the player concentrate on imaginary pitches while practicing the lead arm swings. This will increase the number of repetitions that can be taken in the same period of time.

Coaching Points:

➡ The coach should make sure the player fully extends her lead arm during the swing and follows through properly.

➡ The coach may want to have the players work in groups of three with one hitting, one placing softballs on the tee, and one shagging balls from the net.

➡ The coach should be aware of wrist position (still cocked) just prior to the swing.

Drill #35: Back-Arm Swings

Objective: To teach the hitter to properly extend the back arm.

Equipment Needed: A bat, softballs, a batting tee, and a net.

Description: The player places a softball on the tee and assumes her normal stance, then removes her lead hand from the bat and places it behind her back. She then swings through the ball, driving it into the net approximately 10 feet in front of her. During the drill, she should concentrate on fully extending her back arm and following all the way through. She performs the drill for a specified number of repetitions. The drill can be run without the tee by having the player concentrate on imaginary pitches while practicing the back-arm swings. This will increase the number of repetitions that can be taken in the same period of time.

Coaching Points:

➡ The coach should make sure the player fully extends her back arm during the swing and follows through completely.

➡ The coach may want to have the players work in groups of three with one hitting, one placing balls on the tee, and one shagging balls from the net.

Photo 35.1

Photo 35.2

Drill #36: Both Arms

Objective: To improve hitting technique; to correct flaws in the batting stroke.

Equipment Needed: A bat, softballs, a batting tee, and a net.

Description: The player places a softball on the tee and assumes her normal batting stance. She then hits through the ball while concentrating on all the elements of her swing. This drill is most effective if it is performed immediately after the player has performed a series of practice swings using one of the previously described drills. The repetitive nature of this drill helps the swing become second nature to the hitter. The drill is performed for a specified period of time or until a designated number of repetitions has been completed.

Coaching Point: The coach should carefully observe the players to correct flaws in their swings.

Drill #37: T-Shirt Drill

Objective: To teach hitters the proper position of the hands in relation to the ball.

Equipment Needed: A bat, softballs, a batting tee, and a net.

Description: A softball is placed on the tee, and the hitter assumes her normal batting stance. While taking her stance, she grabs her shirt with both hands in the ready position. She then swings through the ball, releasing her shirt upon full extension at the contact point. This forces the player to keep her hands inside the path of the softball. The drill is performed for a set amount of time or until the desired number of repetitions has been completed.

Coaching Point: The coach should observe the players carefully and correct any flaws in the batting stroke.

Drill #38: Follow-Through Drill

Objective: To improve a hitter's follow-through.

Equipment Needed: A bat, softballs, two batting tees, and a net.

Description: One tee is set up in the strike zone, and the other is placed in the proper follow-through area. A softball is placed on each tee, and the hitter assumes her regular batting stance at an appropriate distance from the tee in the strike zone. The player should concentrate on all the elements of her swing and hit through both balls. If she follows through correctly, she will hit both balls. The drill should be performed for a specified period of time or until a designated number of repetitions has been completed.

Coaching Points:

➡ The coach should observe the players carefully and correct any flaws in their swings.

➡ By varying the placement of the tees, the coach can work on batting strokes designed to hit the ball to different fields.

Drill #39: Instructo-Swing® Drill

Objective: To emphasize the proper relationship between the hands and the barrel of the bat.

Equipment Needed: A bat, softballs, Instructo-Swing®.

Description: The Instructo-Swing® equipment provides a "correct path" (with the barrel of the bat) to emphasize keeping the hands "compact" in the swing phase (Photo 39.1 and 39.3). If the hands "cast out" (Photo 39.2) or "dip" (Photo 39.4), the barrel of the bat will hit the padded bars to provide immediate feedback that the swing is incorrect.

Coaching Point: The coach should observe the players and correct all flaws in their swings.

Photo 39.1 "Correct"—her bat is level.

Photo 39.2 "Incorrect"—she is "casting out."

Photo 39.3 "Correct"—her swinging is compact

Photo 39.4 "Incorrect"—her bat is dipping.

Drill #40: Downward Swing

Objective: To improve the player's ability to swing down through the ball.

Equipment Needed: A bat, softballs, a batting tee, a net, and a chair.

Description: The chair is placed with the seat facing forward so that the back of the chair is behind the hitting zone. The tee is placed just far enough in front of the chair to allow a proper swing with the ball slightly lower than the back of the chair. The hitter assumes her normal batting stance and swings through the ball. To avoid hitting the back of the chair, she must swing slightly downward at the ball. The drill can be performed for a prescribed period of time or until the desired number of repetitions has been completed.

Coaching Point: The coach should emphasize this swing so hitters develop the ability to hit ground balls and line drives and learn not to "uppercut" when swinging.

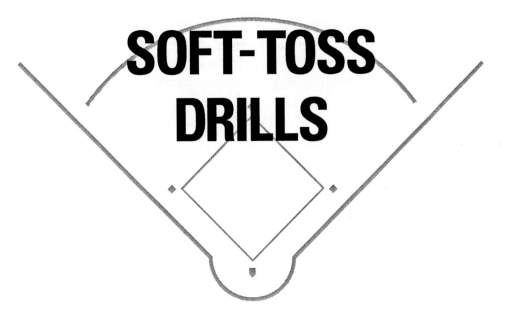

CHAPTER 5

SOFT-TOSS DRILLS

Drill #41: Double-Toss Drill

Objective: To improve hitting technique and reactions.

Equipment Needed: A bat, a home plate, a net, and softball, baseball, and golf ball-size whiffle balls.

Description: This drill involves two players, a batter and a tosser. The batter assumes her normal stance at home plate about 12 to 15 feet in front of the net. The tosser positions herself on one knee, 10 feet in front and slightly to the open side of the hitter. Using two softball-size whiffle balls, she delivers both balls in a slow, underhanded fashion, then quickly calls out "high" or "low" to the hitter. The hitter must react and make contact with the designated ball. After a certain number of hits, the tosser switches to baseball-size whiffle balls. Finally the tosser switches to golf ball-size whiffle balls, forcing the hitter to concentrate harder on the ball.

Coaching Points:

➡ Using two balls forces the hitter to react quickly and delay her swing until the last possible second. Her ability to make quick decisions is also enhanced.

➡ The coach should emphasize maintaining a correct swing despite the speed of the drill.

Photo 41.1 Hitting the "low" ball.

Photo 41.2 Hitting the "high" ball.

Photo 41.3 After the hitter practices hitting the high and low zones, the coach tosses balls at the same time and calls out "high" or "low." The hitter must delay her swing until the last possible second. Upon hearing "high," the hitter swings at the high pitch. Upon hearing "low," the hitter swings at the low pitch.

Drill #42: Soft-Toss Drill

Objective: To improve hitting techniques.

Equipment Needed: A bat, a home plate, a net, and softball, baseball, and golf ball-size whiffle balls.

Description: This drill involves two players, a batter and a tosser. The batter assumes her normal stance at home plate about 12 to 15 feet in front of the net. The tosser positions herself 10 feet in front of the hitter and slightly off to the side. The tosser delivers a slow, underhanded pitch over the plate using a softball-size whiffle ball. The batter drives through the ball and returns to the ready position as quickly as possible for the tosser to deliver another ball. After a certain number of hits, the tosser switches to baseball-size whiffle balls. Finally, the tosser switches to golf ball-size whiffle balls, forcing the hitter to concentrate harder on the ball.

Coaching Points:

➡ The coach may use a third player to shag balls from the net and increase the speed of the drill accordingly.

➡ The coach should observe the players and correct flaws in the swing when necessary, making sure proper technique is not lost in the speed of the drill.

Photo 42.1 Using a *softball*-sized whiffle ball.

Photo 42.2 Using a *baseball*-sized whiffle ball.

Photo 42.1 Using a *golf ball*-sized whiffle ball.

Drill #43: Side-Toss Drill

Objective: To improve hitting techniques.

Equipment Needed: A bat, a home plate, a net, and softball, baseball, and golf ball-size whiffle balls.

Description: This drill involves two players, a batter and a tosser. The batter assumes her normal stance at home plate about 12 to 15 feet in front of the net. The tosser positions herself 10 feet to the side of the hitter. The tosser delivers a slow, underhanded pitch over the plate using a softball-size whiffle ball. The batter drives through the ball and returns to the ready position as quickly as possible, and the tosser delivers another ball. After a certain number of hits, the tosser switches to baseball-size whiffle balls. Finally, the tosser switches to golf ball-size whiffles, forcing the hitter to concentrate harder on the ball.

Coaching Points:

➡ Positioning the tosser to the side of the hitter forces her to wait longer to swing, and can be an effective method of improving timing at the point of contact.

➡ The coach should observe the hitters and correct flaws in the swing when necessary.

Drill #44: Back-Toss Drill

Objective: To improve the hitter's ability to wait on a pitch.

Equipment Needed: A bat, a home plate, a net, and softball, baseball, and golf ball-size whiffle balls.

Description: This drill involves two players, a batter and a tosser. The batter assumes her normal stance at home plate about 12 to 15 feet in front of the net. The tosser positions herself five to six feet behind and slightly to the open side of the hitter's stance. The tosser delivers a slow, underhanded pitch over the plate using a softball-size whiffle ball. The hitter does not watch the tosser. She should keep her head down, concentrate on the strike zone, and react to the pitch, swinging through the ball and driving it into the net. She returns to the ready position as quickly as possible and the tosser delivers another pitch. After a certain number of hits, the tosser switches to baseball-size whiffle balls. Finally, the tosser switches to golf ball-size whiffle balls, forcing the hitter to concentrate harder on the ball.

Coaching Points:

➡ Positioning the tosser to the rear of the hitter forces her to wait on the pitch before swinging.

➡ The coach should emphasize maintaining a fundamentally correct swing despite the speed of the drill. Be sure that the hitter doesn't lunge forward to "catch up" with the ball.

Drill #45: Above-Toss Drill

Objective: To improve hitting technique and reactions.

Equipment Needed: A bat, a home plate, a net, a chair, and softball, base-ball, and golf ball-size whiffle balls.

Description: This drill involves two players, a batter and a tosser. The batter assumes her normal stance at home plate about 12 to 15 feet in front of the net. The chair is placed in front and to the open side of the batter. The tosser stands on the chair, making certain she is clear of where the bat head comes through the strike zone. The tosser holds a softball-size whiffle ball above her head, she drops the ball down through the strike zone. The hitter does not watch the tosser. She should keep her head down, concentrate on the strike zone, and react to the pitch, swinging through the ball and driving it into the net. She returns to the ready position as quickly as possible and the tosser delivers another pitch. After a certain number of hits, the tosser switches to baseball-size whiffle balls. Finally, the tosser switches to golf ball-size whiffle balls, forcing the batter to concentrate harder on the ball.

Coaching Points:

➡ Tossing the balls from above the hitter forces her to react quickly and wait until the last possible second before swinging. This improves reaction time and bat speed through the strike zone.

➡ The coach should observe the players and make corrections in their technique where necessary. Be sure the hitter doesn't bend at the hip or knees (excessively) to "catch up" with the ball dropping through the strike zone.

CHAPTER 6

TIMING & RHYTHM DRILLS

Drill #46: Hip-Thrust Drill

Objective: To teach a player to properly use her hips while hitting.

Equipment Needed: A bat, softball-size whiffle balls, a home plate, and a net.

Description: A batter assumes her normal stance at home plate 12 to 15 feet in front of the net. A tosser positions herself 10 feet in front and slightly to the open side of the hitter. Using soft, underhanded tosses, she delivers pitches into the strike zone. Before each delivery by the tosser, the hitter snaps her hips open, keeping her hands back. She is then in a hitting position with her hips open before she swings at the ball. This forces the hitter not to swing before her hips open. As the toss arrives, the hitter executes the proper swing to take the ball to the opposite field, up the middle, or to the power field.

Coaching Point: The coach should emphasize maintaining a fundamentally correct swing, placing particular emphasis on the relationship of the hip thrust to the hands.

Photo 46.1

Drill #47: Show Ball

Objective: To develop a hitter's ability to react quickly and pick the ball up out of the pitcher's hand.

Equipment Needed: A bat for each hitter and a softball for the pitcher.

Description: Three hitters are spaced far enough apart that their swings will not hit each other. They all assume their normal batting stances facing the same pitcher. The pitcher places both hands and the ball behind her back and randomly decides whether or not to place the ball in her throwing hand. As she comes around to the release point, the hitters must begin the stride and pick up the ball in her hand. If the ball is not in her hand, the hitters continue their stride, keeping their hands back. If the ball is in the pitcher's hand, the hitters swing as though the pitcher actually released the ball.

Coaching Point: The coach should emphasize that the ability to pick the ball up quickly at the release point will improve the batters' ability to recognize strikes.

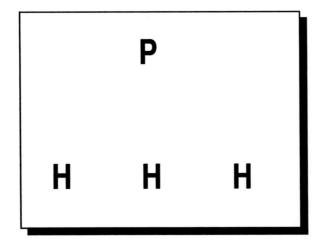

Drill #48: Double-Pump Toss Drill

Objective: To develop the hitter's timing and ability to hit change-ups.

Equipment Needed: A bat, a home plate, a net, and softball, baseball, and golf ball-size whiffle balls.

Description: This drill involves a batter and a tosser. The batter assumes her normal stance at home plate 12 to 15 feet in front of the net. The tosser positions herself on one knee, 10 feet in front and slightly to the open side of the hitter. Using softball-size whiffle balls, she delivers a slow, under-handed pitch. The hitter concentrates on executing a fundamentally sound swing and drives the ball into the net. As the drill progresses, the tosser randomly double-pumps between pitches, forcing the hitter to keep her balance and weight back. The double-pump simulates a change-up. The hitter should return to the ready position quickly after each swing. After a certain number of pitches, the tosser switches to baseball-size whiffle balls, and then to golf ball-size whiffle balls.

Coaching Point: The coach should observe all elements of the batter's swing and make corrections where necessary, placing particular emphasis on keeping the hands and weight back when reacting to the change-up.

Drill #49: Bounce Toss Drill

Objective: To develop the hitter's timing and ability to keep her hands and weight back.

Equipment Needed: A bat, a home plate, tennis balls, and a net.

Description: A batter assumes her normal stance at home plate 12 to 15 feet in front of the net. A pitcher positions herself 10 feet in front and slightly to the open side of the batter and bounces the tennis ball so that it rises over the strike zone after one bounce. The hitter should execute a fundamentally correct swing and drive the ball into the net. The bounce forces the hitter to wait on the ball until it rises into the strike zone.

Coaching Points:

➡ The coach should observe all elements of the swing and make corrections when necessary, placing particular emphasis on keeping the hands and weight back when reacting to the slow pitch.

➡ The hitter should use a slight cocking motion (load—which occurs in stride phase. The lead elbow should move slightly back to the midline of the body) as the tennis ball is in the downward phase of the bounce. As the tennis ball is coming up, the batter keeps her hands back until the ball arrives in her strike zone.

➡ The coach should emphasize that the elbow and wrists remain cocked in the loading phase (stride phase).

Photo 49.1

Drill #50: Double-Machine Drill

Objective: To develop a batter's ability to hit pitches in various locations.

Equipment Needed: A bat, softballs, a home plate, and two pitching machines.

Description: Two pitching machines are set up so that one pitches low and outside and the other pitches high and inside. The batter assumes her normal batting stance at home plate. The machines are set to stagger the delivery of the balls. The batter uses the proper swing to take the low-outside pitch to the opposite field, and adjusts her next swing to pull the high-inside ball. The machines can be set to throw any combination of pitches the coach desires. If a player has a significant weakness in a particular pitch location, the coach may wish to use only one machine and concentrate on that location.

Coaching Points:

➡ The coach should emphasize executing the appropriate swing for each particular pitch.

➡ This drill can also be conducted with one machine at (60-65 MPH for elite players) and the other machine at 45-50 MPH, in order to simulate the change-up pitch.

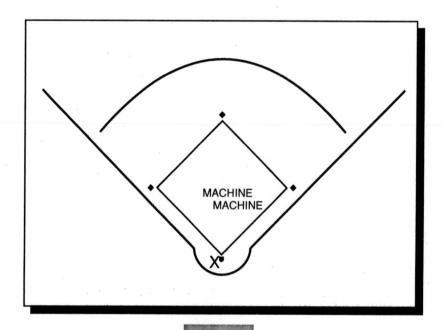

Drill #51: Colored-Ball Drill

Objective: To improve the hitter's reactions and concentration.

Equipment Needed: A bat, two colors of softball-size whiffle balls, a home plate, and a net.

Description: A batter assumes her normal stance at home plate 12 to 15 feet in front of the net. The tosser positions herself 10 feet in front and slightly to the open side of the hitter. The tosser designates which color ball is "live" and rapidly delivers soft, underhanded tosses over the plate. The hitter can only swing at the proper-colored ball, and should return to the set position quickly to be ready for the next toss.

Coaching Points:

➡ The coach should emphasize making quick decisions, waiting on the pitch, and keeping the weight and hands back.

➡ The coach should emphasize maintaining a fundamentally correct swing despite the speed of the drill.

➡ The coach may vary this drill where green designates an "inside" pitch and the player calls out "go." The red ball represents an "outside" pitch and the player calls out "flow" (The tosser should hold the colored ball behind her back until she releases the pitch).

Drill #52: Good Toss—Bad Toss

Objective: To improve the hitter's knowledge of the strike zone; to teach the hitter to lay off bad pitches.

Equipment Needed: A bat, softball-size whiffle balls, a home plate, and a net.

Description: A batter assumes her normal stance at home plate 12 to 15 feet in front of the net. A tosser positions herself in front and slightly to the open side of the hitter. Using soft, underhanded tosses, she delivers random bad pitches mixed in with good strikes. The batter should swing only at the strikes, driving the ball into the net and quickly returning to the ready position.

Coaching Points:

➡ This drill should be performed quickly to enhance the hitter's ability to make quick decisions and discriminate between good and bad pitches.

➡ The coach should emphasize maintaining a fundamentally correct swing despite the speed of the drill.

Drill #53: Spot Toss Drill

Objective: To improve a hitter's ability to hit pitches in various locations.

Equipment Needed: A bat, softball-size whiffle balls, a home plate, and a net.

Description: A batter assumes her normal stance at home plate 12 to 15 feet in front of the net. The tosser positions herself 10 feet in front and slightly to the open side of the hitter. Using soft underhanded tosses, she delivers pitches to a specific spot in the strike zone. The hitter takes the pitch to the appropriate field, executing the proper swing for the pitch location, and quickly returns to the ready position.

Coaching Points:

➡ The coach may wish to have the tosser change the location of the pitches randomly or in a set pattern. If a hitter has a weakness in a certain pitch location, the tosser can concentrate on that area of the plate.

➡ The coach should observe the players and emphasize executing fundamentally correct swings.

CHAPTER 7

LIVE HITTING DRILLS

Drill #54: Machine Work

Objective: To give the players as much hitting practice as possible in a short period of time.

Equipment Needed: A bat, softballs, a home plate, a batting cage or backstop, and a pitching machine.

Description: Using a pitching machine saves time as well as strain on the pitchers' arms. The machine can be set up in the batting cage for individual hitters, or on the field for the entire team. The coach should set the machine to the desired pitch speed and location and have the batters rotate, each taking a certain number of swings. Those players not batting can field or shag balls, or work with the coach on another skill.

Coaching Points:

➡ The coach can also set two machines side by side, each throwing to a different location at a different speed.

➡ The coach should remember that the machine cannot simulate live pitching completely.

➡ The coach should observe the hitters and make corrections where necessary.

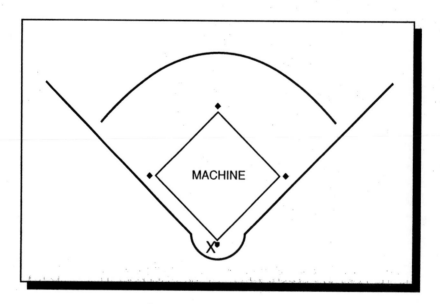

Drill #55: UTM Drill

Objective: To develop a batter's ability to hit the ball up the middle.

Equipment Needed: A bat, softballs, a home plate, and cones.

Description: To avoid the necessity for a catcher, the coach should position the home plate in front of a fence or net to stop any balls the hitter may miss. The cones should be positioned at the back of the infield on either side of second base to define the middle. The drill involves a batter and a pitcher, with more players positioned on defense at shortstop, second base, and centerfield if the coach desires. The hitter assumes her normal stance at the plate and the pitcher throws from the rubber. The drill is performed at full speed with the batter trying to hit a hard ground ball or line drive up the middle between the cones.

Coaching Points:

➡ The coach should emphasize proper timing and concentrating on hitting the top half of the ball.

➡ For safety's sake, a machine may be substituted for the pitcher.

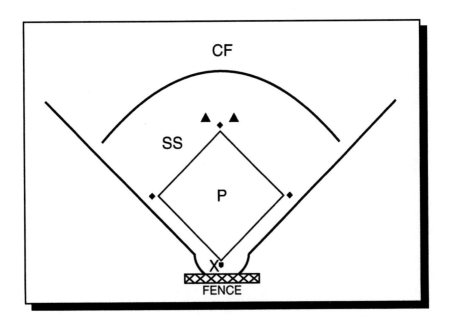

Drill #56: One Ball-One Strike Scrimmage

Objective: To provide live hitting, baserunning, and defensive practice for the entire team at the same time.

Equipment Needed: A softball field, catcher's gear, gloves, softballs, and bats.

Description: The coach should divide the team into two squads by position so that the group in the field will be playing defense in their natural positions. The team at bat organizes its batting order as it would in a regular game. All hitters come to the plate with a one ball-one strike count. The scrimmage is run as a regular game with the teams changing sides each half inning. The drill continues for as many innings as the coach desires.

Coaching Points:

➡ The coach should stop the scrimmage at her discretion to correct errors.

➡ The coach may have teams change sides after six or nine outs to save time.

➡ The coach may create specific game situations by placing runners on base even if they do not hit safely.

➡ If the coach is working on contact/line drive hits, fly outs should be counted as two outs.

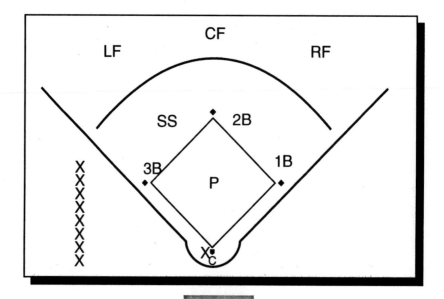

Drill #57: Live Hitting with Non Pitchers

Objective: To provide live hitting practice; to simulate game situations.

Equipment Needed: A bat, softballs, a home plate, and a batting cage or net.

Description: If a batting cage is available, this drill requires only two players: a batter and a partner serving as a pitcher. The batter assumes her normal stance. Her partner pitches from 30 feet in front of her, and throws as many pitches as necessary to give the batter the designated number of bunts and swings. Standing closer than the normal pitching distance aids the partner if she is not actually a pitcher. It also forces the hitter to decide more quickly if the pitch is in or out of the strike zone.

Coaching Points:

➡ This drill allows players to practice hitting live pitching while allowing the coach to work with other members of the team on other skills.

➡ Additional players may be added to shag balls if a batting cage is not available.

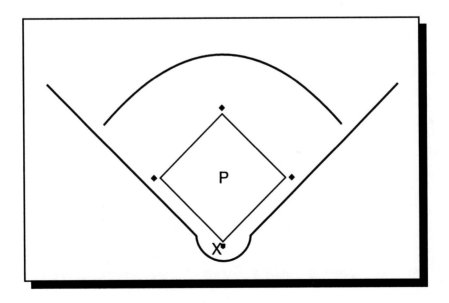

Drill #58: Stride-Correction Drill

Objective: To eliminate common batting stroke problems.

Equipment Needed: A bat, softballs, a home plate, and a batting cage or net.

Description: This drill is not conducted at full speed. It requires a batter, a catcher, and a pitcher, who tosses softballs to the hitter. The hitter assumes her normal batting stance at the plate. The pitcher positions herself five or six feet to the open side of the hitter. On the catcher's command, the hitter takes a short stride of four to five inches at a 45-degree angle toward home plate. She places her weight lightly on the toe of her front foot. At this point, the pitcher tosses the ball into the strike zone. The hitter should concentrate on maintaining her balance and completing her swing. This helps hitters avoid dropping their hands, stepping "in the bucket," and overstriding, and helps increase the hitter's ability to hit to the opposite field.

Coaching Point: The coach should encourage the batter to hit the ball hard and emphasize maintaining balance throughout the swing.

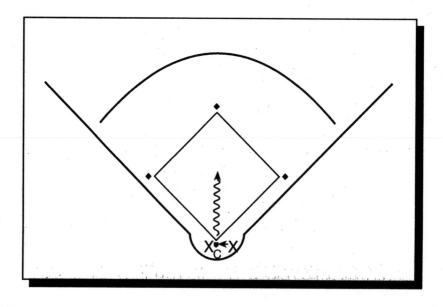

Drill #59: Half-Ball Hitting

Objective: To improve the batter's concentration so she can hit the ball in the air or on the ground at will.

Equipment Needed: A bat, softballs, a home plate, and a batting cage or net.

Description: This drill involves a batter, a catcher, and a pitcher. The hitter assumes her normal batting stance at home plate. The catcher provides the pitcher with a target that she varies from pitch to pitch to cover all areas of the strike zone. The catcher may also wish to change the type of pitch being thrown if the pitcher is able to execute accurately. The hitter should try to pick the ball up at the release point and decide whether to hit the ball on the ground or in the air. Without changing her swing, the hitter concentrates on hitting the top half of the ball for a ground ball or the bottom half of the ball for a fly ball.

Coaching Points:

➡ The coach should emphasize to the hitters that they should not change their swings to produce the fly or ground ball, but restrict their target to the appropriate half of the ball.

➡ The coach may create specific game situations by placing runners on base even if they do not hit safely.

➡ If the coach is working on line drives, the player should work on getting on top of the rise ball and get the bottom half of the down ball.

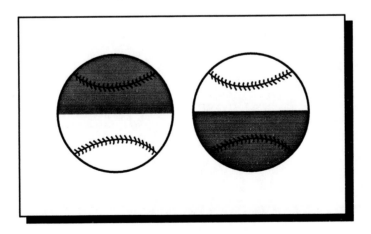

Drill #60: Hitting Behind the Runner

Objective: To develop a hitter's ability to hit to the opposite field; to increase bat control.

Equipment Needed: A bat, softballs, a home plate, and a fence or net.

Description: To avoid the necessity for a catcher, the coach should position the home plate in front of a fence or net. The drill involves a batter, a pitcher, and a fielder. The hitter assumes her normal stance at the plate. The pitcher is positioned 30 feet in front of the plate, and the fielder positions herself approximately 20 feet from the hitter to the opposite field at a 45-degree angle. The pitcher delivers a full-speed toss that the hitter attempts to hit hard on the ground directly to the fielder. The fielder quickly returns the ball to the pitcher, who delivers the next pitch. This creates an enlarged, harder game of pepper.

Coaching Points:

➡ The coach should emphasize swinging from the inside out and concentrating on the top half of the ball. This will increase the hitter's ability to drive the ball hard on the ground and to the opposite field.

➡ The key to this drill is the player must allow the ball to get deeper in the strike zone.

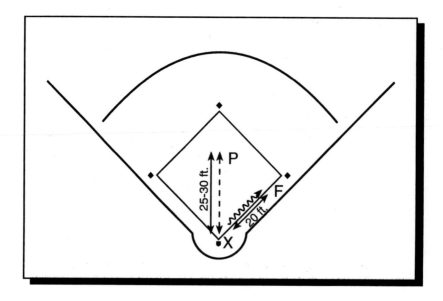

CHAPTER 8

BUNTING
DRILLS

Drill #61: Live-Squeeze Drill

Objective: To improve a player's ability to execute suicide and safety squeeze bunts; to practice baserunning and defense.

Equipment Needed: An infield, catcher's gear, bats, and softballs.

Description: This drill involves the entire team and is run at full-speed. The pitcher, catcher, and first and third basemen assume their normal defensive positions. The rest of the team forms a hitting line down the third base line. The coach places the last hitter in line on third base as a runner. The pitcher should vary the speed, type, and location of her pitches. As the pitcher begins her wind up, the coach yells out the type of bunt to be executed ("suicide" or "safety"). The hitter and third base runner react accordingly. Defensive players take appropriate action, and the bunter attempts to beat out the throw to first. After running out the bunt, the hitter assumes the third-base running position and the third-base runner goes to the end of the hitting line.

Coaching Points:

➡ The coach should rotate pitchers, catchers, and infielders so everyone gets bunting and baserunning practice.

➡ The coach may award two points to hitters and runners who accomplish the squeeze successfully and deduct a point from the score of those who do not. The player with the highest total wins, and the rest sprint the bases.

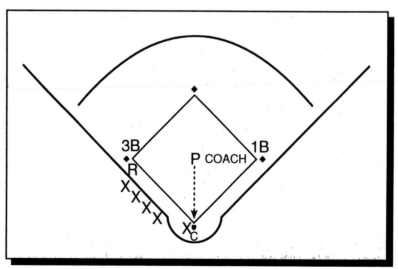

Drill #62: Competition Bunting

Objective: To improve bunting techniques.

Equipment Needed: A bat, softballs, gloves, and towels.

Description: The coach should divide the team into groups of four. One player begins the drill as a hitter, the second as a pitcher, and the third and fourth as infielder-shaggers on either side of the pitcher. The groups should set up in front of a fence, which will serve as a backstop. The towels are used to designate the foul lines (tighter target areas may be designated). To improve her accuracy, the pitcher positions herself 30 feet in front of the hitter, who uses her glove to simulate home plate. The drill is performed in two rotations with each player assuming each position twice. During the first rotation, the pitcher uses a half to three-quarter speed delivery. The batter attempts to bunt the ball down either base line, and earns one point for each successful attempt. Pop ups, foul balls, and missed bunts earn nothing. Each player gets a designated number of bunts in each round. During the second round, the pitcher increases to three-quarter to full-speed deliveries. The player with the most points wins, and the other three sprint the bases.

Coaching Point: The coach should rotate among the groups encouraging friendly competition and correcting flaws.

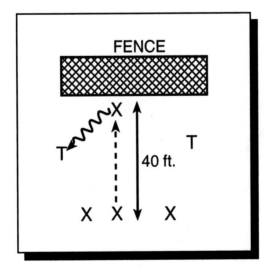

Drill #63: Offense-Defense Bunting Game

Objective: To improve bunting techniques and accuracy; to practice defensive skills.

Equipment Needed: An infield, catcher's gear, bats, bases, softballs, and four cones.

Description: This drill can involve the entire team or a portion of the team. The cones are used to mark off two-foot wide target zones down the first- and third-base lines. A pitcher, catcher, and four infielders assume their normal defensive positions. The rest of the players line up along the third-base line and act as hitters. The pitcher throws at approximately three-quarter speed, and the hitter attempts to bunt them all fairly. To create a competitive atmosphere, the hitter is awarded one point for putting the ball in play, and two points if it dies in the target zone. The hitter earns an extra point for beating the bunt out, and loses a point if she is thrown out. The extra point earned for hitting the target zone is hers to keep even if she gets thrown out. Defensive players earn a point for throwing the runner out at first. The coach should rotate the defensive players so everyone gets a chance to bunt. The player with the most points wins, and the rest run sprints.

Coaching Point: As skill levels progress, the coach may choose to run this drill with the pitcher operating at full-speed and varying the type, speed, and location of her pitches.

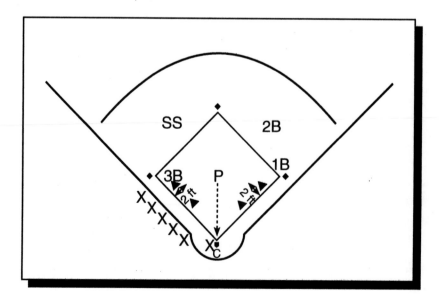

Drill #64: Bunting Scrimmage

Objective: To practice bunting skills and techniques; to practice defending the bunt.

Equipment Needed: Everything necessary to conduct a full game.

Description: The coach should divide the team into two complete squads. The drill is conducted exactly like an intra-squad game except that teams may use only the bunting game when at bat. All types of drag bunts, sacrifice bunts, and fake and swing away bunts can be used, as well as squeeze bunts, bunting in first and third situations, and faking and hitting behind the runner. Score is kept and the winners run half as many sprints as the losers do. The players should man their own coaching boxes, and the coaches and manager serve as umpires.

Coaching Point: The coach may decide whether to stop the game to correct errors or hold a short meeting after the game is over.

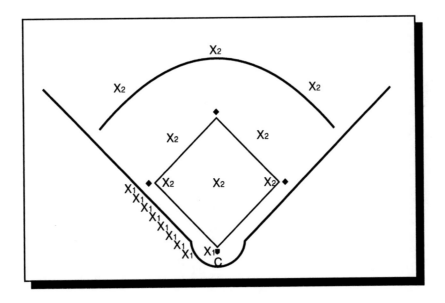

Drill #65: Fake Bunt and Swing Away

Objective: To practice the fundamentals of sacrifice bunting; to teach the fake sacrifice and hit away maneuver.

Equipment Needed: A bat, gloves, and softball-size whiffle balls.

Description: The team should be divided into pairs, with as many pairs of players participating at one time as the coach desires. The use of whiffle balls eliminates the risk of injury from a hard throw or a bunt-and-slashed ball. The hitter uses her glove to simulate home plate and assumes her regular batting stance. The pitcher stands 25 to 30 feet away and delivers fastballs to the hitter. The hitter practices sacrificing down each imaginary baseline for a designated number of attempts, and then executes the same number of fake sacrifice-and-slash hits. She should concentrate on trying to hit the fake bunt hard on the ground past an imaginary drawn-in infielder. After the designated number of attempts, the pitcher and hitter switch roles.

Coaching Point: The coach should circulate around the groups and correct mechanics where necessary. This is a good drill to use early in the season to provide individual instruction on proper techniques.

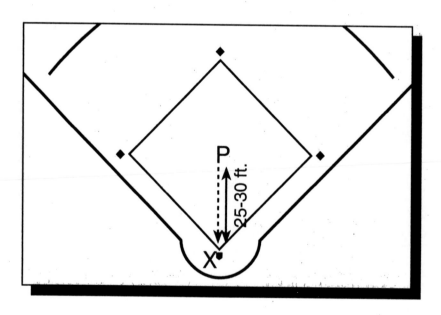

Drill #66: Toss Bunting

Objective: To improve bunting fundamentals.

Equipment Needed: Softballs and a bat.

Description: A hitter assumes her normal stance at home plate. A tosser positions herself on one knee 10 to 12 feet in front of the hitter and delivers soft, underhanded tosses over the plate. The hitter should attempt a designated number of sacrifice bunts and then switch to drag bunts. After a designated number of bunts, the two players gather the balls and change positions.

Coaching Point: This is a good drill to use early in the season to work on bunting skills. It also lends itself well to indoor activity in case of inclement weather. As many pairs of players can perform the drill at one time as desired.

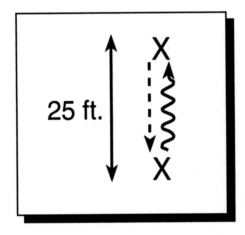

Drill #67: Target Bunting

Objective: To develop the player's ability to bunt accurately to any specified area.

Equipment Needed: Bats, softballs, a rope, and two bags or buckets.

Description: The rope is placed in a semicircle approximately 15 feet from home plate. The drill involves a pitcher, a catcher, and as many hitters as the coach desires. To speed up the drill, the pitcher and catcher have buckets beside them to hold balls. Each hitter begins the drill in her regular stance. Concentrating on picking up the ball at the release point, she attempts to bunt the pitch so that it stops inside the area designated by the rope. She gets only two attempts. If she successfully bunts either one, she runs it out to first base. If she fails to bunt either one, she sprints around the bases before returning to the end of the line. The pitcher should simulate a game situation by varying the type, speed, and location of her pitches.

Coaching Points:

➡ Defensive practice can be incorporated into the drill by adding a first, second, and third baseman. The defense should field the bunt and attempt to throw the runner out at first.

➡ The drill can be made more difficult by requiring the hitter to bunt up the first or third base line. Towels can be used to designate the target areas.

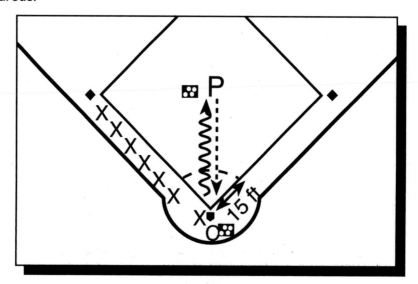

Drill #68: Double Bunt Drill

Objective: To practice bunting techniques.

Equipment Needed: Bats, softballs, catching gear, a protective screen, and four buckets or bags.

Description: The coach divides the team into two squads, each with a pitcher and catcher. One squad sets up at home plate and the other at second base. The protective screen is set up at the rubber with one pitcher on each side. Once the pitcher delivers to home plate, the other squad throws to second base. Each pitcher and catcher has a bag or bucket to hold balls. A player from each squad bunts the ball and runs it out. Players bunting from the plate run to first, and players bunting from second run to third. The players should run through the bag as they would in a game situation. After running out the bunt, they go to the end of the opposite hitting line. All types of bunts can be practiced during this drill.

Coaching Point: The coach may use towels to designate target areas for the bunter.

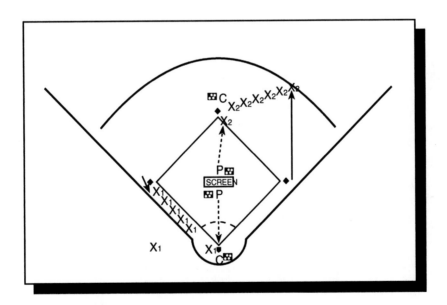

Drill #69: Three-Player, Bunt-Shagger

Objective: To improve bunting techniques.

Equipment Needed: A bat, softballs, and gloves.

Description: The coach should divide the team into groups of three. One player begins the drill as a hitter, the second as a pitcher, and the third as a shagger. The groups should set up using a fence as a backstop. Two gloves are used to simulate the foul lines (tighter target areas may be designated), and the object is for the hitter to bunt the ball between the two gloves. The pitcher works from 30 feet in front of the hitter and throws at three-quarter speed. The shagger retrieves the bunted balls as quickly as possible. After the hitter has completed a designated number of sacrifice bunts, the players rotate. After one rotation is complete, the players perform a second rotation practicing drag bunts.

Coaching Points:

➡ Where skill levels allow, the pitchers should vary the type and location of their pitches.

➡ The coach may specify that half of the bunts be practiced down the first base line and the other half down the third base line.

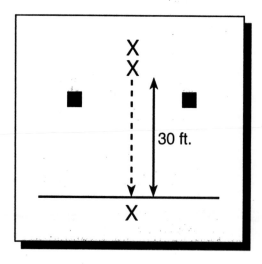

Drill #70: Four-Player, Bunt-Pitch-Shagger

Objective: To improve bunting techniques.

Equipment Needed: A bat, softballs, gloves, and towels.

Description: The coach should divide the team into groups of four. One player begins the drill as a hitter, and the other three serve as pitcher-shaggers. The groups should set up using a fence as a backstop. The hitter uses a glove to simulate home plate. The pitcher-shaggers form a line 30 feet in front of the hitter. The towels should be set up to designate the foul lines or any other target area the coach desires. The first pitcher in line delivers her pitch and retrieves it at full speed, no matter what the outcome of the attempted bunt. The second pitcher delivers her pitch as quickly as possible. The pitchers continue to throw and shag in rotation until the hitter has practiced a designated number of bunts. The first pitcher in line then becomes the hitter. The drill continues until all four players are finished bunting.

Coaching Points:

➡ Where skill levels allow, the pitchers should vary the type and location of their pitches.

➡ The coach may specify that half of the bunts be practiced down the first base line and the other half down the third base line.

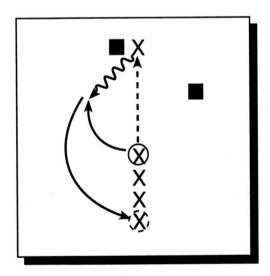

CHAPTER 9

BASE RUNNING DRILLS

Drill #71: Sign Drill

Objective: To improve the player's ability to recognize and interpret offensive signs; to improve conditioning.

Equipment Needed: An outfield area.

Description: The coach should divide the team into two squads. The squads should form two rows facing each other about 40 yards apart. Each squad should have a coach or manager giving signs. The coaches give signs to their own group at the same time. The runners leave their imaginary base according to the sign that was given, and then sprint toward the other team. All players run at once, taking care not to hit each other as they pass. They receive the next sign from the other coach and proceed as before. The number of repetitions is determined by the coach.

Coaching Points:

➡ Offensive signs should be reviewed daily and before every game. This is a good drill to use after a game in which signs were missed.

➡ The player that recognizes the signal first sprints to the other side. The coach repeats her signal sequence until the players see the sequence.

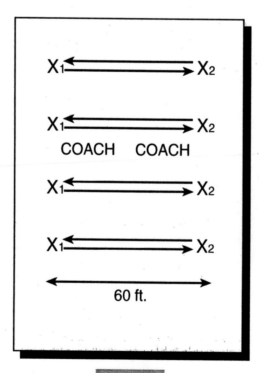

Drill #72: Star with Two

Objective: To improve the runner's ability to round the bag properly.

Equipment Needed: An infield with secured bases.

Description: The coach should divide the team into two equal groups. Each group should form a single-file line on opposite sides of first base along the base line. The first player in each line should be approximately 40 feet from the bag. On the coach's signal, the first player in each line starts running and rounds the bag as if she is heading for second base. If their turn is too wide, the players will bump into each other. The next player in line should begin her run as the previous player makes her turn. After making the turn, the player goes to the end of the opposite line.

Coaching Points:

➡ The coach may have players begin the drill at a jog and work up to full-speed baserunning.

➡ The coach should emphasize touching the inside of the bag with the outside foot when making the turn.

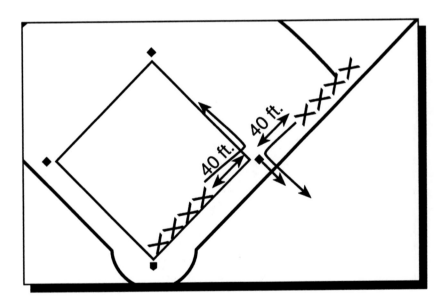

Drill #73: Star with Four

Objective: To improve the runner's ability to round the bag properly.

Equipment Needed: An infield with secured bases.

Description: The coach should divide the team into four equal groups. Each group should form a single-file line on one side of second base—one along each baseline, one in centerfield, and one between the base and the pitcher's mound. The first player in each line should be approximately 40 feet from the bag. On the coach's signal, the first player in each line starts running and rounds the bag as if she is heading for the next base. If their turn is too wide, the players will bump into each other. The next player in each line begins her run as the previous player makes her turn. After making the turn, the player goes to the end of the line to the left of her original line.

Coaching Points:

➡ The coach may have players begin the drill at a jog and work up to full-speed baserunning.

➡ The coach should emphasize touching the inside of the bag with the outside foot when making the turn.

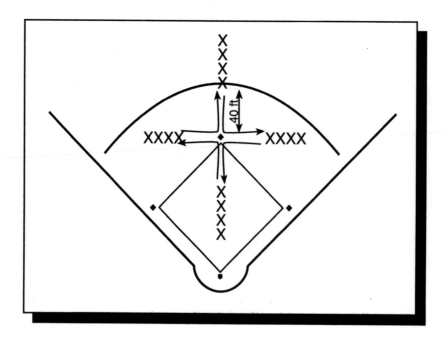

Photo 73.1 Players contact the "inside" corner (the corner pointing to the pitcher's mound) of the base.

Photo 73.2 Ideally, players should hit the inside of the base with their outside foot when making the run.

Photo 73.3 If the player's turn is too wide, the players will bump into each other.

Drill #74: Tag Ups

Objective: To improve timing when tagging up to advance after a fly ball is caught.

Equipment Needed: A field with secured bases, a softball, and a glove.

Description: The drill begins with a runner at each base, including home plate. The rest of the players form a single line at home plate to wait their turn. The coach positions herself in the mound area and each of the runners takes a normal lead off her base. The coach throws a high pop-up which she catches herself. The runners retreat to their own bases, tag up, and time their break toward the next base to coincide with the coach's catch. Other coaches and players make sure the runners do not leave early. The runner at third goes to the end of the waiting line at the plate when she scores. The other runners stay on the base they advanced to and the drill continues.

Coaching Points:

➡ To involve more players at once, other stations can be set up using simulated bases in the outfield areas.

➡ To add realism to the drill, the coach can add three outfielders who take their normal positions and catch fungos from the coach.

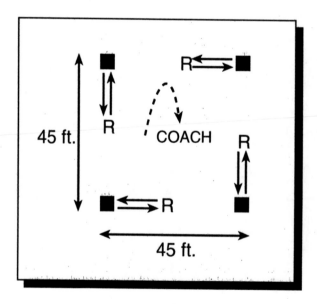

Drill #75: Breaking Up the Double-Play

Objective: To teach players the baserunning and sliding techniques used in breaking up the double-play.

Equipment Needed: Outfield areas, tennis balls, and two simulated bases for each area used.

Description: The coach should divide the players into two or three squads, each with three infielders to act as the first baseman, second baseman, and shortstop. A coach or manager should be with each group. Players form a single line behind first, and the first runner in line takes her normal lead off the bag. The second baseman and shortstop are at their normal double-play positions, and the first baseman holds the runner on. The coach is positioned near the pitcher's rubber. The coach "hits" and the runner breaks for second, checking to find the ball. The coach delivers a hand-thrown ground ball to any of the fielders. The runner concentrates on where the shortstop is setting up to throw. Staying in the baseline, she prepares to slide slightly to the side of the bag from which she thinks the shortstop will throw. On hits to first, she delays sliding until the last second, hoping the throw from first will hit her in the back. On hits to second and short, she should try to anticipate the pivot.

Coaching Point: The coach should stress sliding to avoid being hit in the face with the throw to first. She should also emphasize that the hard slide into second is an attempt to hinder the throw to first, never an attempt to injure an opponent.

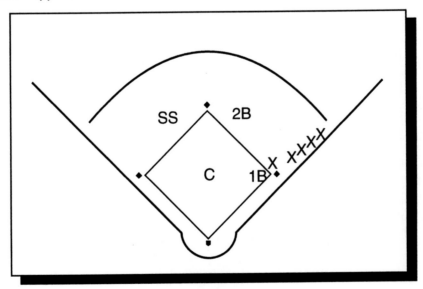

Drill #76: Box to First Drill

Objective: To improve the hitter's ability to get out of the batter's box quickly.

Equipment Needed: Four bats and four bases.

Description: The team is divided into groups of four. A smaller version of an infield is set up with four bases approximately 45 feet apart. One player begins at each base, positioning herself as if the base were home plate and assuming her normal batting stance. The coach stands on the "mound" and delivers an imaginary pitch. Each hitter swings through, concentrates on getting out of the box quickly and explosively, and runs to the next bag. She picks up the bat at that bag and the drill continues. Each player gets a designated number of full swings, and then practices exploding from the box after executing imaginary drag and sacrifice bunts.

Coaching Points:

➡ Several miniature diamonds can be set up so that more players can participate at the same time.

➡ The coach should emphasize getting out of the box quickly and explosively.

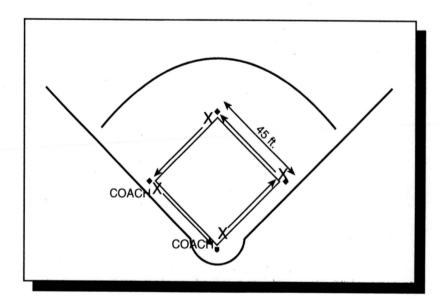

Drill #77: Run Through First Drill

Objective: To teach hitters the techniques used in correctly running from home through first base.

Equipment Needed: Three home plates and three first bases.

Description: The coach divides the team into three groups who form lines behind the three home plates. Three bases are set up at regulation distance from the plates. The first player in each line steps up to the plate and assumes her regular batting stance. She executes an imaginary swing and concentrates on leaving the box quickly and explosively. She should focus on running to a spot about five yards past first base to help her realize the importance of running all the way past the bag. As she approaches first, she looks down to make sure she touches the bag, then turns her head to the right to see if there has been an overthrow that might allow her to take second. She then returns to the end of the line to wait for her next turn.

Coaching Points:

➡ The coach should emphasize looking down at the bag and glancing over the right shoulder checking for overthrows to instill good habits in the players.

➡ This can be turned into a competitive drill by having the three groups run it as a relay race.

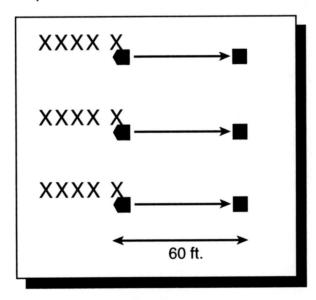

Drill #78: Sprint-Jog-Sprint-Jog

Objective: To improve a player's ability to round a bag correctly and explosively; to improve conditioning.

Equipment Needed: An infield with secured bases.

Description: Players form a line at home plate. The first player takes her regular stance, swings at an imaginary pitch, and sprints toward first. She sprints through first base, making sure she touches the bag and glances over her shoulder for overthrows. As she passes the bag, the next player in line begins the drill. Players jog to second base. As they approach second, they concentrate on rounding the bag properly and explode in a full sprint to third. They round the bag properly and ease up to jog home. After a designated number of trips around the bases using this pattern, they sprint two bases and jog the next two. The drill continues up the ladder until they sprint three and jog three, and finally, sprint all four and jog all four.

Coaching Point: The coach should emphasize setting up properly to round each bag, executing the proper footwork, and exploding toward the next base.

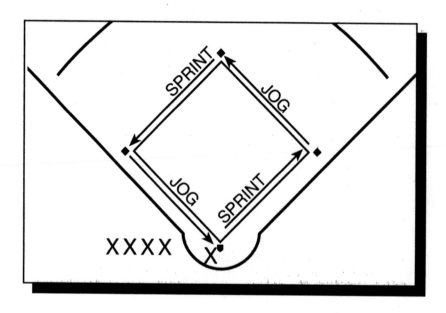

Drill #79: Sprint Relays

Objective: To improve baserunning skills and conditioning.

Equipment Needed: A field with secured bases.

Description: The coach should divide the team into two squads of approximately equal speed. One squad begins the drill at home plate and the other at second base. Players can position themselves in any order they like, but are not allowed to change positions in line once they are set. On the coach's command, the first runner in each group sprints around all the bases and tags the next runner on her team. When one team overtakes the other, the drill is over and the losing team pays a penalty chosen by the coach.

Coaching Point: The coach should emphasize setting up properly to round each bag, executing the proper footwork, and exploding toward the next base. If the teams are equal in speed, the team using the best baserunning technique will usually win.

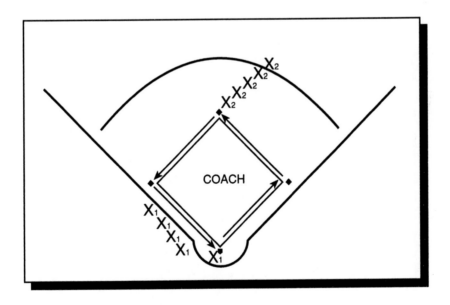

Drill #80: Game Situation Drill

Objective: To improve baserunning skills; to improve coordination between base coaches and runners.

Equipment Needed: A field with secured bases, softballs, and a fungo bat.

Description: The drill begins with a defensive team in the field at their normal positions and base coaches at first and third. The remaining players serve as runners. A coach or designated player hits fungos. The first runner in line reacts to the fungo, running the bases at full speed and taking directions from the base coaches regarding whether she should take the next base or hold up. As many game situations can be created as the coach wishes. This drill is an excellent way to practice the team's normal game day signals. Offensive and defensive teams should switch sides halfway through the drill.

Coaching Points:

➡ The coach hitting the fungos should create as many game situations as possible, forcing the base coaches and runners to make quick decisions.

➡ The coaches should designate when the players pick up the coach when they are the primary and secondary runner.

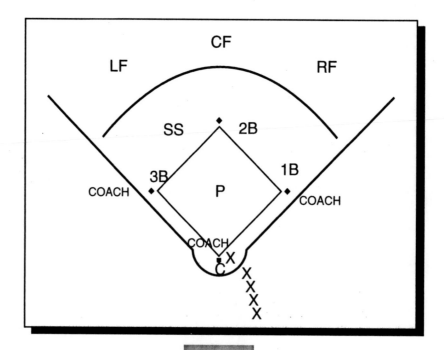

Drill #81: Lead Off-Jump Starts

Objective: To teach players to get a proper lead off the bag and a good jump off the pitcher.

Equipment Needed: A field with secured bases.

Description: The coach divides the team into four groups who form lines at home plate, first, second, and third. A pitcher is on the mound throwing imaginary pitches from her normal wind-up. The hitter assumes her normal stance and practices getting a good jump and sprinting through first. The other three runners get a good lead off their bags and try to get the best jump off the pitcher they can. The runner on third breaks to the plate for a suicide squeeze, and the runners on first and second break for a steal, run and hit, or run and bunt. Each player then goes to the end of the line at the base to which she was running. After one or two rounds, the players practice breaking as if a safety squeeze or sacrifice bunt were being executed.

Coaching Points:

➡ The coach may choose to call out which play is being executed so she can make sure runners are using the proper techniques.

➡ The coach should explain the proper distances to lead off based on which base they are on.

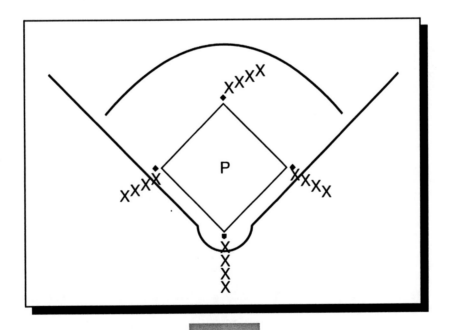

Drill #82: Four-in-One Drill

Objective: To work on all phases of baserunning; to improve conditioning.

Equipment Needed: A field with secured bases and a bat.

Description: The coach should divide the team into four equal groups with one stationed at home plate and one at each of the bases. The first player in line at the plate takes the bat and assumes her normal stance in the batter's box. The first players in line at the other bases take a normal lead off the bag. At the coach's command, all four runners take action. The hitter at the plate swings at an imaginary pitch and sprints through first base, making sure she touches the bag and checks for overthrows. The runner at third sprints all the way through the plate, and the runners at first and second advance to the next base, rounding the bag and holding up. These four players continue the drill for a full trip around the bases and then go to the end of their original lines. The next runner in each line then begins the circuit.

Coaching Points:

➡ The players should practice getting out of the box after a drag or sacrifice bunt as well as a full swing.

➡ Runners approaching the plate should take instructions from the next player in that line about whether to slide or remain standing. Runners going into second and third can be instructed to execute different types of slides.

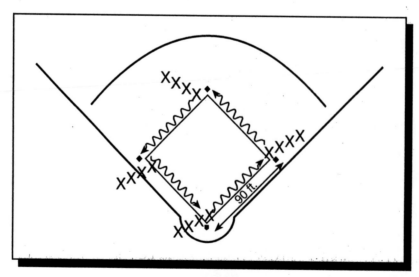

Drill #83: Tag Game

Objective: To improve a player's ability to start quickly and accelerate toward the next bag.

Equipment Needed: A field with secured bases.

Description: The coach should divide the team into two equal squads. One group forms a line at third base and the other at first. The first player in each line is positioned seven to eight feet off the bag. The second player in line starts from the bag. The object of the drill is for the second runner to catch the lead runner before they reach the next base. They begin running on the coach's command. If the lead runner reaches the next base first, she is awarded one point and allowed to continue as the baserunner. If she is caught, the second runner gets the point and moves into the lead runner position. After each player has had two chances to be the lead runner, the player with the most points wins. The losers suffer penalties determined by the coach.

Coaching Point: The coach should emphasize quick reactions and starts while making sure the players do not jump the gun.

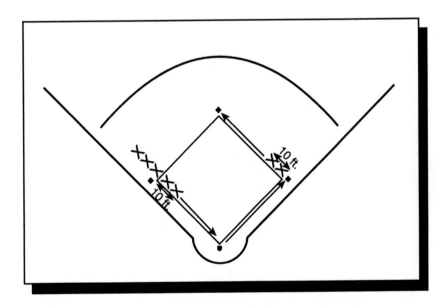

Drill #84: Reaction Drill

Objective: To improve a player's reaction time.

Equipment Needed: A field and enough bases (or simulated bases) to create four simulated diamonds.

Description: The coach should split the team into groups of five, each with at least one pitcher. Three infields are set up (on the dirt and grass area) with the bases about 40 feet apart and a group is assigned to each field. The pitcher positions herself where the mound would be, and the other players are positioned on the four bases. Each player takes a normal lead off her base, and the pitcher simulates a delivery to the plate. The runners get the best jump they can off the pitcher and break toward the next base, using either a track or crossover step according to the preference of the coach. The players accelerate to full speed, then ease up and jog to the next base. The drill continues for a set period of time or until a designated number of circuits has been completed.

Coaching Point: The coach should emphasize the importance of proper footwork in base stealing. She should circulate among the groups to observe the players and make corrections in their footwork if necessary.

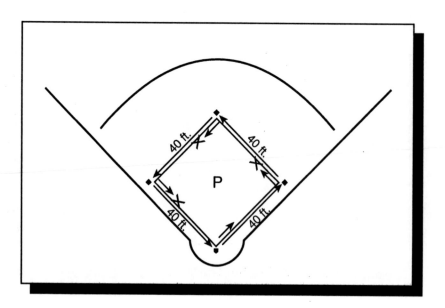

Drill #85: Wild Pitch Break Drill

Objective: To improve a baserunner's ability to make quick decisions on a wild pitch or passed ball.

Equipment Needed: A field with a backstop and secured bases, catcher's gear, and softballs.

Description: This drill requires a pitcher and catcher, shortstop, and first, second, and third basemen in their regular positions. Baserunners are stationed at first and second. Other runners form a line at first base to wait their turn. The runners get a good lead, and the pitcher delivers to the plate. She intentionally throws the ball in the dirt, forcing the catcher to attempt to block the ball with her body. The runners break and must decide quickly if it is safe to take the next base. If the runners break for the next base, the catcher attempts to throw out one of the runners. The regular first- and third-base coaches help the runners decide when and how to slide into the bag. After the play, the runner who started at first remains at second and the next player in line leads off first.

Coaching Point: While primarily a baserunning drill, this is also excellent defensive practice. The catcher can also try to catch a runner who made a bad decision in a run down.

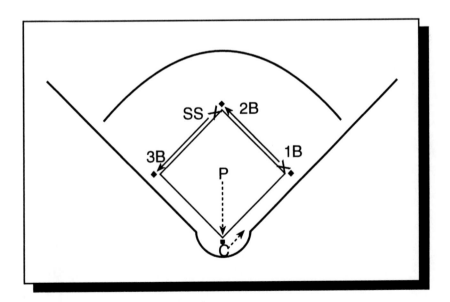

Drill #86: Timed Baserunning

Objective: To improve a player's ability to get out of the batter's box quickly.

Equipment Needed: Bats, softball-size whiffle balls, bases, and stopwatches.

Description: The coach should divide the team into four equal groups. Four stations are set up, each with two bases spaced regulation distance apart. The first player in each line takes a bat and assumes her regular batting stance, positioned so the other base is where first base would normally be. The next player in line gets down on one knee about six feet in front of the hitter and lobs a whiffle ball over the plate. The batter hits the ball and gets out of the box to first base as quickly as she can. A coach or manager times her effort with a stopwatch. The hitter runs all the way through first, making sure she touches the bag and checks for an overthrown ball. Charts should be kept on each player and posted in the locker room.

Coaching Points:

➡ The drill can be moved to a regular diamond with secured bases. Players can be timed stealing second, third, or home off a pitcher simulating a throw.

➡ To improve conditioning as well as practice baserunning, players can be timed rounding all four bases.

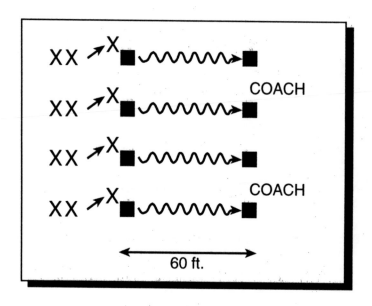

Drill #87: Mirror Game

Objective: To improve a player's footwork and reaction time.

Equipment Needed: Enough bases (or simulated bases) to accommodate the entire team.

Description: The coach should divide the team into pairs. Each pair should have two bases spaced regulation distance apart. The first player takes an 8- to 10-foot lead off one base with the second player four or five feet behind her on the base path. The lead runner makes the decision to break for the next base or back to the first one. Whatever the lead runner decides, the second runner tries to beat her to her destination. After a designated number of repetitions, the players switch roles.

Coaching Point: The coach should emphasize proper footwork and a quick, explosive first step.

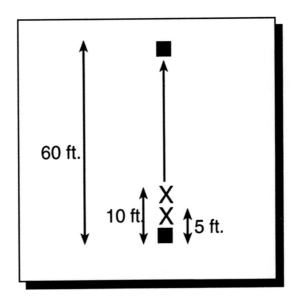

Drill #88: Hit-and-Run Dodge Ball

Objective: To improve the player's ability to go from first to third on a hit-and-run without being struck by a batted ball.

Equipment Needed: A field with secured bases and softball-size whiffle balls.

Description: The coach should divide the team into two equal squads. One squad lines up at third base and the other at first. The first player in each line takes a normal lead. The second player in each line acts as the "hitter" and positions herself about 20 feet inside and slightly up the line from the runner. The runners break on the coach's command as if executing the hit-and-run. They should look to find the ball, and the hitters attempt to stride the runners with a hard ground ball or low line drive. Runners must avoid the batted ball, round second, and sprint into third.

Coaching Point: The coach should observe the footwork on the break and when rounding second base, and make corrections where necessary.

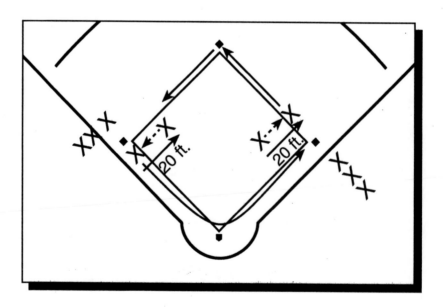

Drill #89: Working the Pickle

Objective: To practice getting out of a run down.

Equipment Needed: Four bases (or simulated bases) and tennis balls.

Description: The coach should divide the team into two squads. Each squad has two bases spaced regulation distance apart. Two players in each group serve as defensive infielders, and the first player in each line is the baserunner. The baserunner should break hard toward a base. If the infielder makes an early throw, the baserunner stops, pivots, and sprints for the opposite base. Baserunners should stay in the base line and in line with the player about to receive the throw. This path increases her chances of being hit in the back with the throw. If possible, she should run into a defensive player in the base line, prompting an interference call. The coach should rotate other infielders into the drill at designated intervals.

Coaching Points:

➡ Although this is a baserunning drill, the coach should emphasize using the correct defensive techniques when executing the run down.

➡ The coach should teach players when to prolong the run down (allowing the runner behind to advance, double steal) and use the same drill to practice those situations.

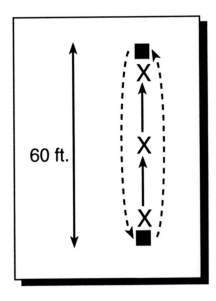

CHAPTER 10

SLIDING DRILLS

Drill #90: The Crab Walk

Objective: To begin the process of teaching correct, safe sliding techniques.

Equipment Needed: An outfield area, simulated bases, and sliding mats (or cardboard).

Description: The coach should divide the team into four groups, each working at a station equipped with a simulated base and a sliding mat. The mat is placed two feet in front of the base. Players form a single line six to eight feet from the mat. The first player in line assumes the crab walk position, facing up with her back parallel to the ground. Her legs are underneath her at about a 90-degree angle, and her hands are on the ground for support. She crab walks toward the mat as quickly as she can. As she reaches the mat, she tucks one leg under, straightens the other leg, and slides toward the base. She quickly replaces the mat and returns to the end of the line.

Coaching Point: This is the first step in learning the proper fall for sliding. The crab walk provides a way for the coach to teach the proper position of the runner's legs and hands without having the players take too big a fall.

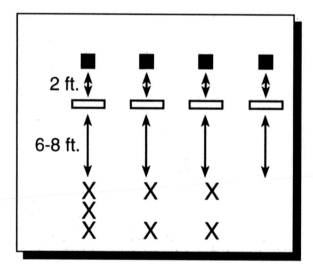

Drill #91: The Bear Crawl

Objective: To continue the process of teaching correct, safe sliding techniques.

Equipment Needed: An outfield area, simulated bases, and sliding mats (or cardboard).

Description: The coach should divide the team into four groups, each working at a station equipped with a simulated base and a sliding mat. The mat is placed four feet in front of the base. The players form a line 10 to 12 feet away from the mat. The first player in line assumes the bear crawl position on all fours, facing the ground with her hands and feet under her. She bear crawls as quickly as she can toward the mat. As she reaches the mat, she throws her legs under her toward the base, one leg tucked under and the other extended straight toward the bag. The momentum of her forward thrust will carry her to the bag. She quickly replaces the mat and returns to the end of the line.

Coaching Points:

➡ The bear crawl provides more speed and gives the player a better feel for how to fall when sliding. It is still much safer for the beginner than sliding from the running position.

➡ The coaches should circulate among the groups to check for proper leg and hand positioning.

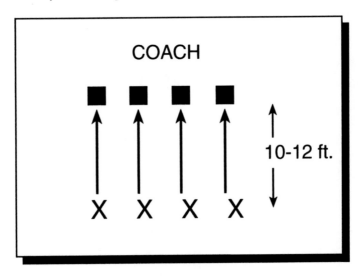

Drill #92: Slip and Slide

Objective: To continue the process of teaching correct, safe sliding techniques.

Equipment Needed: A well-watered outfield area and simulated bases.

Description: The coach should require the players to wear game pants (or sweat pants) for this drill. The players are split into four groups, each working at a station equipped with a simulated base. The runners form lines at each station about 30 feet from the base. The first runner slides through the wet grass to the bag. The wet grass makes the slide easier and also creates a fun atmosphere. The drill should begin at three-quarter speed and progress to full speed.

Coaching Points:

➡ This drill is safer than sliding in dirt or dry grass and is a logical step in the progression of teaching sliding techniques. The coach should emphasize maintaining the proper sliding technique despite the fun atmosphere.

➡ The beginner should slide without spikes at first.

Drill #93: No-Hands Sliding

Objective: To improve sliding mechanics and safety.

Equipment Needed: An outfield area, simulated bases, and empty water cups.

Description: The team should be divided into four groups, each working at a station equipped with a simulated base. Players form a line approximately 30 feet from the base. They hold empty water cups in each hand to help them keep their hands closed. The drill begins at half to three-quarter speed and progresses to full speed. The players slide into the bag, concentrating on keeping their hands closed and above their heads and their legs in the proper position.

Coaching Points:

➡ In addition to the hands, the coach should emphasize correct leg positioning and remind the players to keep the figure four position.

➡ The beginner should slide without spikes at first.

Drill #94: The Limbo

Objective: To teach players the importance of flattening out when sliding.

Equipment Needed: An outfield area, simulated bases, and toilet paper.

Description: The coach should divide the team into four groups, each working at a station equipped with a simulated base. Two players stretch a length of toilet paper about three feet above the ground three feet in front of the bag. The players start about 30 feet away and slide into the bag, flattening out to slide under the toilet paper. If they hit the toilet paper, they are not in the proper sliding position. The drill begins at half to three-quarter speed and progresses to full speed as players master the timing and techniques of proper sliding.

Coaching Point: The coach should circulate among the players, emphasizing keeping the hands closed and the legs in the figure four position, as well as extending the upper body back while the chin is placed on the chest. This will avoid the slider's head hitting the ground when the upperbody momentum goes backwards.

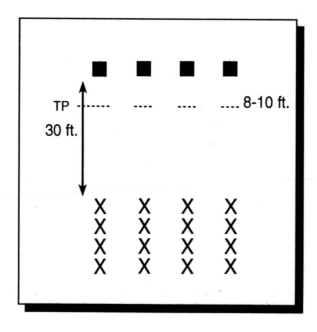

Drill #95: The Stand-Up Slide

Objective: To practice the correct mechanics of the stand-up or pop-up slide.

Equipment Needed: An outfield area and simulated bases.

Description: This drill is performed in two phases. The first involves the players working individually to practice the mechanics of the stand-up slide. Each player assumes the proper figure four sliding position on the ground. At their own speed, the players practice shifting their weight forward until it is all on the front leg. The weight shift will help the players to stand up. In the second phase of the drill, the players are split into four groups, each working at a station equipped with a simulated base. Players line up about 30 feet away from the bag and practice pop-up slides under the coach's supervision. The drill should begin at half to three-quarter speed and progress to full speed as the players master the proper timing and techniques of stand-up sliding.

Coaching Point: After working on the grass with loose bases, the drill should move to an infield with secured bases.

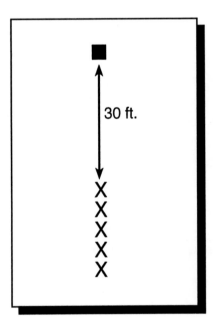

Drill #96: Reaction Slides

Objective: To practice pop-up, bent-leg, hook, or head-first slides.

Equipment Needed: An infield with secured bases, softballs, and bats.

Description: Players form one line at home plate. A coach is stationed in the first base coach's box, and a coach or manager is in shallow left field with a bag of softballs. The first player in line assumes her normal batting stance. On the coach's command, she swings at an imaginary pitch and gets quickly out of the box, sprinting to first. The first base coach signals the player to take second. As the player rounds the bag, she looks for the ball. The coach in left field will either drop the ball or pull it into her body as if throwing behind the runner. The runner reacts accordingly. If the ball is dropped, she races to second and executes a bent-leg, hook, or pop-up slide. If a throw is feigned, she retreats to first and executes a head-first slide.

Coaching Point: The coach may designate which slide to practice at second base.

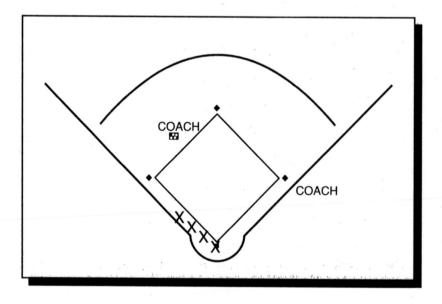

Drill #97: Four-Slide Drill

Objective: To practice head-first, bent-leg, pop-up, and hook slides.

Equipment Needed: An outfield area and simulated bases.

Description: A diamond should be set up on the grass using four simulated bases. The team should be split into four groups with a group at each base. The coach or manager stands in the middle of the group as if on the rubber. The first player in each line takes a normal lead off her base. Runners practice a head-first slide at first, a bent-leg slide at second, and a pop-up slide at third. Runners going into home practice a hook slide. After each base, the runners take a new lead and wait for the simulated pitch. When a runner slides into her original base, she goes to the end of the line and the next player begins the circuit.

Coaching Points:

➡ The coach may choose to move this drill to an infield with secured bases.

➡ Coaches should be positioned at each base to observe the players and make corrections where necessary.

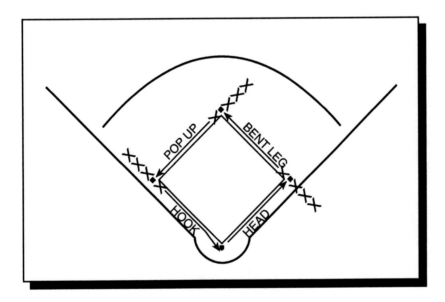

CHAPTER 11

MENTAL DRILLS

Drill # 98: Positive Pictures

Objective: To employ mental imagery to enhance player performance.

Description: While warming up before practices and games, players replay in their minds images of events with which they have personally had success on the previous day or during the prior week. These images help reinforce each player's perception that she possesses the skills and attributes essential for top-flight performance. Thinking about how she *has* played can have a positive impact on how she *will* play.

Coaching Points:

➡ Coaches should emphasize to their players the fact that each athlete has all the skills that she needs to be all that she wishes to be as a performer.

➡ Coaches should encourage their players to recall and focus on the positive aspects of their recent performances.

Drill #99: Knowing Your Lights

Objective: To enhance the ability of the players to achieve and sustain a positive emotional state of mind.

Description: This drill is designed to allow each player to be better aware of her personal state of mind during the course of the game and to be able to adjust her mindset accordingly. Collectively, the emotional roller coaster that a player may ride during a game is divided into three zones—each assigned a different colored light. When a player is confident and assured, she has a *green* light. The athlete has a *yellow* light if she is feeling somewhat apprehensive about her ability to perform at a satisfactory level. For example, she may have swung and missed at the first pitch and is starting to question her talent. Finally, if her emotional state is in severe disruption (i.e., she is crashing and burning), she has a *red* light.

Coaching Point: Coaches should remind and encourage their athletes to employ the techniques described in Drills #98, #100, and #101 to enhance their emotional state whenever they fall to either a yellow or red light status.

Drill # 100: Know Your Focal Point

Objective: To reinforce the player's perception that she can perform at an acceptable level.

Description: When a player is in her red light (emotional) zone, she is encouraged to picture a positive focal point and remind herself how hard she has worked to maximize her playing ability. Given her expended efforts, this drill is designed to provide the athlete with a personal reminder that she *can* perform well on the field.

Coaching Point: Coaches should encourage their players to focus on positive points, and in the process adopt a "can do" attitude.

Drill #101 Mental Verbiage

Objective: To employ selected self-trigger words to enhance an athlete's emotional state and level of performance.

Description: In this drill, players are constantly recreating positive images in their minds by talking to themselves in their heads. Examples of the mental verbiage that a player could employ in this instance would include, "my hands are quick," "the barrel of my bat is fast," "I can see the ball exceptionally well," etc.

Coaching Point: Coaches should remind their players of the positive impact that self-trigger words can have on performance.

Sue Enquist is the head softball coach at UCLA. The 2001 season marks Enquist's 13th campaign as head coach of the Bruin softball program. It is her 22nd year as part of UCLA's softball coaching staff and her 26th year of involvement with the program as either a coach or player.

This is Enquist's fifth season as the sole head coach for the Bruins. Enquist took over that role beginning with the 1997 season, following the retirement of longtime Bruin mentor Sharron Backus. The two served as co-head coaches from 1989-96.

Before being named co-head coach, Enquist coached nine seasons (1980-88) as an assistant under Backus. Enquist spent just one season away from the program, 1979, immediately after completing her eligibility as a member of UCLA's 1978 AIAW Championship team. Enquist was the tournament's leading hitter as UCLA won its first softball National Championship.

Since that time, Enquist has been a member of the UCLA coaching staff for all of its eight NCAA Championships, the most of any school. The NCAA brought women's sports under its umbrella beginning with the 1981-82 academic year. UCLA won that inaugural NCAA softball championship, and has since played in 14 championship games, winning titles in 1982, '84, '85, '88, '89, '90, '92 and '99. The 2000 Bruins fell just short of a second consecutive NCAA Championship, losing in the Championship game to Oklahoma.

As a centerfielder under Backus from 1975-78, Enquist became the prototypical player for Bruin softball in terms of attitude, desire and will to win. UCLA's first softball All-American, Enquist led the Bruins in doubles three times and twice led UCLA in batting average and triples.

Enquist established the UCLA career batting average record with an impressive .401 mark, and is still the only Bruin to complete her career with a batting average over .400. Enquist's No. 6 jersey was retired on April 29, 2000, becoming the third number in Bruin softball history to be retired, joining the No. 16 of Lisa Fernandez and No. 1 of Dot Richardson.

A three-time ASA All-American for the Raybestos Braketts, Enquist helped lead that team to four ASA National Championships in 1976, '77, '78 and '80. She also enjoyed success as a player at the international level, earning gold medals at three National Sports Festivals, the 1978 World Championships, and the 1979 Pan American Games.

Enquist earned her bachelor's degree in kinesiology from UCLA in 1980. A native of San Clemente, CA she is an avid surfer and currently resides in Huntington Beach, CA.

A list of Enquist's accomplishments and honors:

- The Bruin coaching staff was chosen as the 2000 National Fast-pitch Coaches Association (NFCA) Pacific Region Coaching Staff of the Year. It is the third time that Enquist has received this honor, as she was named Regional Coach of the Year in 1991 and '92.
- Enquist was named the National Coach of the Year in 1992.
- She is a two-time Pac-10 Coach of the Year, earning the honor in 1995 and '99.
- Enquist was the first softball inductee to the UCLA Hall of Fame, as a member of the Class of 1993. There are currently five Bruin softball players in the Hall of Fame, including Enquist, Debbie Doom, Dot Richardson, Sheila (Cornell) Douty and Tracy Compton.
- As one of eight softball coaches chosen to work with the U.S. National Team, Enqusit was involved in the preparation of the gold medal winning U.S. Olympic Team for the Summer Games in Atlanta, GA, the inaugural Games for softball as an Olympic medal sport.
- Enquist was the head coach of the 1993 Olympic Festival Championship team, and coached the USA Pre-Elite National Team in July, 1994.
- She was also a member of the coaching staff for the gold medal winning 1994 world Championship team, contested in Canada.
- Enquist was among the list of "20th Century Bruins" put together by UCLA Magazine at the close of 1999.

- Since Enquist's elevation to co-head coach in 1989, 27 players have earned All-American honors in forty separate instances.

- Enquist was UCLA's first All-American, earning the honor in 1978 after being named All-Region in 1976, '77 and '78.

- She coached seven former Bruins who participated with the gold medal winning 2000 U.S. Olympic Team—Christie Ambrosi, Jennifer Brundage, Sheila Cornell Douty, Lisa Fernandez, Stacey Nuveman, Dot Richardson and alternate Amanda Freed.

- All three of UCLA's current assistant coaches (Kelly Inouye-Perez, Fernandez, Gina Vecchione) are UCLA graduates and were coached by Enquist during their Bruin careers.

- She was inducted into the Capistrano Unified School District Hall of Fame in October 2000.

- Enquist has 1,006 wins in her Bruin softball career as a player and coach, combined.

James A. Peterson, Ph.D., FACSM, is a sports medicine consultant and author who resides in Monterey, California. Among the more than eighty books he has written are *Finding the Winning Edge* with Bill Walsh and *Competitive Leadership* with Brian Billick. A graduate of the University of California at Berkeley, he served as a full professor on the faculty at the United States Military Academy at West Point for almost twenty years. In 1990, he accepted a job as the Director of Sports Medicine for StairMaster Sports/Medical Products, Inc.—a position he held for five years.

In addition to his efforts with authoring books, Dr. Peterson has written over 150 published articles on a variety of sports medicine, conditioning, and coaching topics. He has given presentations at more than 200 coaching clinics worldwide and has appeared on a number of nationally televised programs, including ABC's Nightline, The CBS Evening News, and ABC's Good Morning America. Finally, since 1992, he has been an active, volunteer fund-raiser for the Make-a-Wish Foundation®.